Virtual Learning Communities

SRHE and Open University Press Imprint
General Editor: Heather Eggins

Current titles include:

Catherine Bargh *et al.*: *University Leadership*
Ronald Barnett: *Beyond all Reason*
Ronald Barnett: *The Limits of Competence*
Ronald Barnett: *Higher Education*
Ronald Barnett: *Realizing the University in an Age of Supercomplexity*
Ronald Barnett and Kelly Coate: *Engaging the Curriculum in Higher Education*
Tony Becher and Paul R. Trowler: *Academic Tribes and Territories (2nd edn)*
Neville Bennett *et al.*: *Skills Development in Higher Education and Employment*
John Biggs: *Teaching for Quality Learning at University (2nd edn)*
Richard Blackwell and Paul Blackmore (eds): *Towards Strategic Staff Development in Higher Education*
David Boud *et al.* (eds): *Using Experience for Learning*
David Boud and Nicky Solomon (eds): *Work-based Learning*
Tom Bourner *et al.* (eds): *New Directions in Professional Higher Education*
John Brennan *et al.* (eds): *What Kind of University?*
Anne Brockbank and Ian McGill: *Facilitating Reflective Learning in Higher Education*
Stephen D. Brookfield and Stephen Preskill: *Discussion as a way of teaching*
Ann Brooks and Alison Mackinnon (eds): *Gender and the Restructured University*
Sally Brown and Angela Glasner (eds): *Assessment Matters in Higher Education*
Burton R. Clark: *Sustaining Change in Universities*
James Cornford and Neil Pollock: *Putting the University Online*
John Cowan: *On Becoming an Innovative University Teacher*
Sara Delamont, Paul Atkinson and Odette Parry: *Supervising the PhD*
Sara Delamont and Paul Atkinson: *Research Cultures and Careers*
Gerard Delanty: *Challenging Knowledge*
Chris Duke: *Managing the Learning University*
Heather Eggins (ed.): *Globalization and Reform in Higher Education*
Heather Eggins and Ranald Macdonald (eds): *The Scholarship of Academic Development*
Gillian Evans: *Academics and the Real World*
Andrew Hannan and Harold Silver: *Innovating in Higher Education*
Lee Harvey and Associates: *The Student Satisfaction Manual*
David Istance, Hans Schuetze and Tom Schuller (eds): *International Perspectives on Lifelong Learning*
Norman Jackson and Helen Lund (eds): *Benchmarking for Higher Education*
Merle Jacob and Tomas Hellström (eds): *The Future of Knowledge Production in the Academy*
Peter Knight: *Being a Teacher in Higher Education*
Peter Knight and Paul Trowler: *Departmental Leadership in Higher Education*
Peter Knight and Mantz Yorke: *Assessment, Learning and Employability*
Mary Lea and Barry Stierer (eds): *Student Writing in Higher Education*
Dina Lewis and Barbara Allan: *Virtual Learning Communities*
Ian McNay (ed.): *Higher Education and its Communities*
Elaine Martin: *Changing Academic Work*
Louise Morley: *Quality and Power in Higher Education*
Moira Peelo and Terry Wareham (eds): *Failing Students in Higher Education*
Craig Prichard: *Making Managers in Universities and Colleges*
Michael Prosser and Keith Trigwell: *Understanding Learning and Teaching*
John Richardson: *Researching Student Learning*
Stephen Rowland: *The Enquiring University Teacher*
Maggi Savin-Baden: *Problem-based Learning in Higher Education*
Maggi Savin-Baden: *Facilitating Problem-based Learning*
Maggi Savin-Baden and Kay Wilkie: *Challenging Research in Problem-based Learning*
David Scott, Andrew Brown, Ingrid Lunt and Lucy Thorne: *Examining Professional Doctorates*
Peter Scott (ed.): *The Globalization of Higher Education*
Peter Scott: *The Meanings of Mass Higher Education*
Michael L. Shattock: *Managing Successful Universities*
Maria Slowey and David Watson: *Higher Education and the Lifecourse*
Anthony Smith and Frank Webster (eds): *The Postmodern University?*
Colin Symes and John McIntyre (eds): *Working Knowledge*
Peter G. Taylor: *Making Sense of Academic Life*
Richard Taylor, Jean Barr and Tom Steele: *For a Radical Higher Education*
Malcolm Tight: *Researching Higher Education*
Penny Tinkler and Carolyn Jackson: *The Doctoral Examination Process*
Susan Toohey: *Designing Courses for Higher Education*
Paul R. Trowler (ed.): *Higher Education Policy and Institutional Change*
Melanie Walker (ed.): *Reconstructing Professionalism in University Teaching*
Melanie Walker and Jon Nixon (eds): *Reclaiming Universities from a Runaway World*
David Warner and David Palfreyman (eds): *Higher Education Management of UK Higher Education*
Gareth Williams (ed.): *The Enterprising University*
Diana Woodward and Karen Ross: *Managing Equal Opportunities in Higher Education*

Virtual Learning Communities

A Guide for Practitioners

Dina Lewis and Barbara Allan

Society for Research into Higher Education
& Open University Press

Open University Press
McGraw-Hill Education
McGraw-Hill House
Shoppenhangers Road
Maidenhead
Berkshire
England
SL6 2QL

email: enquiries@openup.co.uk
world wide web: www.openup.co.uk

and Two Penn Plaza, New York, NY 10121–2289, USA

First published 2005

A catalogue record of this book is available from the British Library

ISBN 0335 21282 4 (pb) 0335 21283 2 (hb)

Library of Congress Cataloging-in-Publication Data
CIP data applied for

Typeset by RefineCatch Limited, Bungay, Suffolk
Printed in the UK by Bell & Bain Ltd, Glasgow

Dedication

This book is dedicated in memory of Gertrude Carr, who nurtured a wide range of learning communities.

Contents

List of Figures

List of Tables

List of Boxes

Acknowledgements

We would like to acknowledge the help, support and inspiration of all the community members with whom we have worked and participated. In addition we would like to thank all our colleagues who have supported our activities in this field. With special thanks to Colin Guthrie, Bob Hunter, Jennie Headland-Wells, Nancy Rowland and Lynn Saville.

Please note that Chapters 3 and 10 have been developed and built upon previously published work by Barbara Allan.

1
Introduction to Learning Communities

Introduction

This chapter introduces readers to the book and also to the concept of learning communities. It provides an introduction to the authors, their context and approach to this work, and the chapter ends with a brief outline of the book as a whole. The chapter introduces the concept of learning communities and explores their relationships with other types of learning groups. It discusses the role of learning communities in workforce development and the growth of virtual learning communities in recent times. Finally, the benefits of virtual learning communities (VLCs) for individuals, organizations and the wider profession are also outlined in this chapter.

Introduction to the book

This book is aimed at readers who are either involved in or thinking about becoming involved in **virtual** learning communities. You may be a member of a community and thinking about ways of developing its effectiveness. Alternatively, you may be thinking of setting up a strategic infrastructure to support such a group, for example as part of an organizational development programme. You may be a trainer with access to a VLE and an interest in using computer-mediated conferencing as a learning tool to support group-work. The book focuses on the practical skills and theoretical understanding required to encourage the growth of such communities from the perspective of community facilitators and also from the perspective of effective community participants. We also provide guidance on developing models and infrastructures to support strategic approaches to workforce development and partnership working through the formation of learning communities.

We have identified a gap in the knowledge and understanding of strategic planners, senior managers, academics, training managers and trainers in how to establish and run successful learning communities. It seems that everyone is talking about their potential yet in practice very few people have the knowledge and understanding of the underpinning pedagogy to achieve their successful implementation. The enthusiastic aspirations of senior managers and individuals do not usually result in the sustained development of effective learning communities. Practitioners with enthusiasm and technical skills in using learning technologies often lack the pedagogical understanding to support the development of these communities to greatest effect. This book will provide an introduction and practical guide to such an underpinning theoretical framework.

The book will be of interest and relevance to those with a responsibility and/or interest in staff development, such as managers or supervisors of teams and staff groups, personnel officers, trainers or consultants, or other change agents. The content is relevant for those employed in the public, private or voluntary sectors, and will also be relevant to independent workers such as those following portfolio careers where networking and membership of learning communities can offer a means of alleviating potential isolation. In essence the book is a practitioner's guide to facilitating and participating in dynamic collaborative learning communities. This book is based on the authors' experiences of a range of communities as well as their research in this field as indicated below:

- Dina Lewis is a member of a number of professional groups, a steering group for a regional development project, a community of researchers from a wide range of backgrounds in adult learning, community of school governors, Blackboard user group, and others.
- Barbara Allan is a member of a number of different professional groups, for example an e-learning community, a community of women managers, a community of managers in the voluntary sector. From 2000 to 2002 she was a member of an e-learning programme, the MEd. Networked Collaborative Learning, which developed into a learning community. In her private life she is a member of a dog training learning community.
- Dina and Barbara have also worked together as facilitators of virtual learning communities, for example multi-professional groups in universities, multi-professional groups within the NHS, managers working in the steel industry and manufacturing.
- Research into this book has involved visits and discussions with colleagues who are members of other virtual learning communities, for example speech therapists, library and information workers, health professionals, industrialists.
- Further information and examples have been obtained from professional networks and conferences, and also through the growing literature in the field.

We recognize the great potential of virtual communication tools to support new approaches to collaborative learning but do not think it is helpful to focus exclusively on the virtual communities and learning technologies. In our experience the most effective communities are those that use a mixture of face-to-face and virtual interactions, that is, a blended approach. Although the book will offer guidance on learning technologies it is important to emphasize at this stage that our focus is on 'how' to use technology to facilitate approaches to collaborative learning. We firmly believe that community facilitators and participants will be empowered by an understanding of the pedagogy of online learning and without this the technology is of limited use.

Working together on the book

Our approach in working on this book has mirrored the approach we use in our work as members and also facilitators of virtual learning communities and this means that it has been developed on constructivist principles. We have worked together (and also independently) on making sense of our practical experiences in live communities and at the same time linking this with theory. This means that much of the book is written in the first person. It also means that we are not offering a prescriptive approach to facilitating virtual learning communities. We are offering our own experiences (warts and all!) and ideas, and we have located these in the research literature. We hope that you will use the book as a resource and as something that will help you in your own journeys in this fascinating world of virtual learning communities.

The majority of the examples used in this book are based on our own professional practice. Community members have been very willing to share their experiences with us and we thank them for their time and commitment to our work. We have changed their names and also other details so as to maintain their anonymity.

Structure of the book

The first three chapters set the context of virtual learning communities. This chapter introduces readers to virtual learning communities and distinguishes them from learning programmes, communities of practice and communities of interest. It also explores the rise of virtual learning communities and the benefits they bring to individuals, organizations and the wider profession. Chapter 2 provides an introduction to virtual learning communities, their structure and common working practices within communities. This chapter uses a range of examples to illustrate three different models of community. Chapter 3 provides an overview of relevant information and communication technologies (ICTs). This chapter does not explore the technical aspects of ICT but provides an overview of different technologies and explains their potential relevance to virtual learning communities. This chapter considers tools such as e-mail, discussion groups and conferencing software. It also explores the applicability of group communications software and virtual learning environments (VLEs).

The next four chapters are concerned with the realities of community life. Chapter 4 describes the authors' model of the life cycle of a typical community and this is made up of six phases: foundation; induction; incubation; improving performance; implementation; closure or change. These phases are briefly described before the chapter focuses on the foundation and induction phases. Chapter 5 is concerned with incubation; Chapter 6 looks at improving performance, implementation, and closure or change. Each of these chapters takes a similar approach as they illustrate what happens within each phase and provide guidance for community facilitators.

Chapter 7 explores community participation from two different perspectives: community members and facilitators. It covers the following topics: community members – functional roles and responsibilities, skills and attributes of effective members, group and team dynamics; facilitators – roles and responsibilities, skills and attributes of effective facilitators, working with co-facilitators. The chapter concludes with an examination of member and facilitator participation levels.

One of the reasons for many developments in virtual learning communities is the recognition that learning may be viewed as a social activity. This underpinning concept is explored in Chapter 8 and here we have related our own experiences and research findings to the theoretical models of people like Vygotsky and Wenger. This is an important chapter as facilitators of virtual learning communities really need to understand the pedagogical basis of this approach to individual and workforce development.

Our experience is that time is a significant issue for many community members and it is one of the most important factors in determining whether or not individual participants become active and effective community members. As a result we have dedicated Chapter 9 to exploring time-related issues and this chapter also provides facilitators with a range of strategies that may be used to empower the community members to overcome temporal challenges and become actively engaged in their community.

Chapter 10 focuses on working in partnership, which has become an increasingly important way in which multi-professional groups are working together across different organizations. Partnership working can be extremely challenging and, at its best, incredibly rewarding. This chapter outlines some of the main issues associated with partnership working and it also illustrates how virtual learning communities may be used as a means of providing a space for partners to work and learn together.

The final chapter explores different approaches to community evaluation. This is a crucial process as it enables facilitators, managers and sponsors to identify the benefits of the virtual learning community and also to identify areas for change or improvement. This chapter explores traditional tools for evaluation, for example questionnaires and interviews, and it also looks at different approaches for using narrative analysis (based on e-mail, discussion group or conference transcripts) for illuminating individual and whole group experiences.

What are learning communities?

In the past decade there has been a growing interest in learning and professional development in particular, in the development of approaches to enhance the performance of professionals. There has been a paradigm shift from models of education and training where knowledge and skills are transmitted through formal attendance at training sessions to an approach that encourages groups of practitioners to work together to examine, evaluate and construct knowledge and skills relevant to their current professional practice and the context of their particular workplace. It is possible to identify three distinct yet related frameworks for supporting professional development:

- structured learning/training programmes;
- learning communities; and
- communities of practice.

The majority of people are familiar with **structured learning and training programmes** and these are characterized as follows:

- pre-planned with pre-determined aims and learning outcomes;
- programme is often owned by an education or training organization;
- programmes are facilitated by a tutor or trainer who has a responsibility for curriculum content and ensuring that the programme follows its pre-determined course including a set range of activities or tasks;
- clear start and end date;
- differential in power between the learner and the tutor/trainer;
- programmes are often accredited, for example by higher education institutions or professional bodies;
- the learner is sometimes viewed as a 'customer' who consumes the learning.

In some instances the outcomes of traditional learning programmes include the development of a network or community of learners who continue to meet, discuss and work on professional issues over time after the end of a formal taught programme. In the wake of the constructivist movement many educators and trainers are re-examining traditional approaches to learning and training. Tutors and trainers are now seeing the benefits of involving students, stakeholders and trainees in the process of programme design. Tutor-/trainer-determined activities and strategies within clear boundaries of time and space are no longer meeting the needs of many professionals working in the knowledge economy of the twenty-first century. Individuals and organizations are utilizing learning technologies and current ideas about learning and knowledge management to achieve organizational, professional and personal development. Collaborative groups are gathering together to provide mutual support for improving performance in new and dynamic ways, and tutors and trainers are engaging in innovative and exciting ways of facilitating collaborative approaches to learning.

Learning communities are changing the way that we learn and work together. Groups of professionals and practitioners, often from the same or related professional background, are coming together to share ideas and experience and to tackle professional and work-based problems and issues. Brent Wilson and Martin Ryder (1996) define dynamic learning communities as follows:

> In learning communities members share control and everyone learns, including the facilitator or tutor or group leader. Transformative communication is the norm, with both sender and receiver of messages changed by the interaction . . . all participants are engaged in the learning experience.

Transformative learning communities are being established to enable like-minded people or colleagues or professionals with a common or multi-professional interest to work together and to achieve a particular aim or organizational objective. They are often established within organizations as a means of bringing together a creative network of colleagues with a complementary set of knowledge, skills and attitudes to produce dynamic approaches to problem solving, knowledge management and knowledge creation. Sometimes communities develop within or across organizations as the result of a structured programme of study and some communities may be developed as part of a regional commitment to strategic workforce development, or sometimes communities develop as part of an organization's plan to create a critical mass of professionals able to work collaboratively or in partnership to manage change and deal with issues pro-actively.

Many professional development programmes provided by colleges and universities enable individuals from a number of different backgrounds and organizations to form learning communities and benefit from shared perspectives on professional practice or local issues and problems. At the end of a formally structured learning community programme successful learning communities often continue to work together.

Learning communities are usually characterized by the following:

- a shared goal, problem or project;
- shared resources;
- shared membership and leadership;
- commitment to improvement of professional practice;
- collaborative approaches to groupwork;
- learning and development focused on real work-based issues and practice;
- autonomous community members;
- high levels of dialogue, interaction and collaboration;
- information and knowledge sharing;
- knowledge construction;

- knowledge transfer and knowledge exchange;
- use of information and communication technologies.

Any discussion of learning communities is not complete without reference to **communities of practice**. Jean Lave and Etienne Wenger (1991) adopted *communities of practice* as a term to describe how professionals learn through collaborative and supportive social interactions in their seminal book *Situated Learning: Legitimate Peripheral Participation*. They challenged traditional epistemology and received assumptions about the nature of knowledge and learning, and proposed a social theory of learning based on their observations of professionals learning in work-based contexts. Wenger observed learning as an all-encompassing process involving individuals in active participation in the practices of social communities and he proposed that professional individuals construct professional identities in relation to their membership of communities of practitioners, these communities are often informal and unrecognized by employing organizations. Wenger's theories have greatly influenced current managerial thinking and it is difficult to pick up a business publication today without seeing some reference to communities of practice.

Communities of practice are usually characterized by the following:

- common purpose identified by participants;
- shared membership and leadership;
- participants likely to be at different stages in their professional life;
- development of professional practice through apprenticeship;
- acceptance of low levels of participation by new members, that is, legitimate peripheral participation;
- development, creation and management of knowledge within organizations;
- open-ended, not time bound;
- importance of dialogue, interaction and shared narratives.

This book is focused specifically on our experience of working with learning communities. Many of these learning communities have been linked to more formal learning programmes and our experience of learning communities closely relates to the characteristics of communities of practice previously listed. In our experience, the terms learning programmes, learning communities and communities of practice are often used interchangeably and distinctions between these concepts can be confusing and blurred. We acknowledge that there are clear distinctions between the frameworks, however, as our examples throughout the book will demonstrate learning communities are highly complex, living, evolving, changing organisms and we use the term **learning community** loosely. We use it as a generic term to encompass all the collaborative learning groups that we have facilitated and in which we have participated. Our examples include learning communities that could also be described as learning programmes and learning

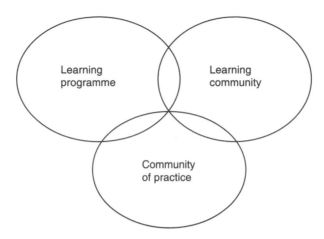

Figure 1.1   Relationships between learning programmes, learning communities and communities of practice

communities that exhibit many of the characteristics of communities of practice. The definition of learning communities that we offer is:

> A learning community is a supportive group of people who come together to collaborate and learn together, they are usually facilitated or guided to achieve a specific outcome or agreed learning objectives.

Figure 1.1 summarizes the relationships between learning programmes, learning communities and communities of practice.

Communities of interest should also be mentioned before we go any further. Communities of interest are large groups or networks, perhaps involving hundreds of people, and they support the dissemination and exchange of information but do not necessarily support collaborative learning processes. They develop when people come together to exchange news or information about a specific topic. Examples include groups that cluster together around their interests in hobbies, technology, education, research fields and specialist work-related practices. E-mail discussion lists are a good example of communities of interest and sometimes a sub-group of such a community may develop into a learning community.

Learning communities in action

Learning communities are located within many professions and employing organizations. They offer formal and informal networking opportunities for individuals to meet and communicate to gain support, guidance and

Table 1.1 Comparison of learning communities and communities of interest

Characteristics	Learning communities	Community of interest
Purpose	To problem solve To improve professional practice To improve the effectiveness of an organization or project To create and expand knowledge	To be informed To share ideas and information To meet up with like-minded people
Membership	People who share a particular interest or passion in a topic People who volunteer or are invited to become a member This may be self-selected or by invitation Membership is likely to be relatively small, e.g. 6–24	Open to people who share a particular interest This is likely to be self-selected People who become subscribers or members of a particular group, e.g. mail list, e-learning programme Membership may be very large, e.g. 12–1000
What holds them together	Passion, commitment, identity with group Personal relationships within the group	Access to information and sense of like-mindedness
Examples	Some groups involved in collaborative project work Professional groups supported by professional organizations Some e-learning programmes	Some discussion groups Newsgroups

information. They offer individuals opportunities to discuss real-life issues and develop new insights, share problems and explore innovative solutions and strategies. They are particularly effective in enabling individuals and groups to identify and explore current issues and problems, particularly those that are pushing on the boundaries of accepted knowledge and practice. They offer a means through which individuals and groups can construct new knowledge and approaches to tackle a whole range of professional and technical issues and problems. Some examples of learning communities that have informed our research are:

- professional teams working within organizations;
- strategic clusters of companies working towards regional economic success;
- professional associations and bodies;
- trade unions;
- multi-professional teams working on improved practices and services;
- interdisciplinary teams working at the cutting edge of their field of knowledge;

- special interest groups;
- practitioners working across traditional professional boundaries.

Learning communities develop for a specific focus or purpose and they may be located around:

- a strategic response to the need for a unified approach to improvement in a sector or geographical region;
- a specific problem or issue such as the need to implement a new system or process within an organization;
- a particular professional group such as librarians or information workers;
- the need to work across professional boundaries and sectors such as initiatives in the health sector involving consultants, nurses, social services and voluntary agencies;
- a dispersed professional group, for example individuals working in isolation across a continent.

Typical learning communities share a range of features. Probably the most important of these is that the members are passionate about their subject or field and feel a commitment towards their community. They will regularly take part in community activities as these are focused on issues, problems and developments that have a direct impact on the participants' work role and context. Learning communities help participants to create, expand, and share knowledge relevant to their professional practice. Members of successful communities are likely to view participation in a community as a significant aspect of their work and feel their membership makes a difference to their ability to perform at work. Effective communities tend to be relatively small, that is 6–24 people; the group should be small enough for members to form relationships and get to know each other well. In some cases the community also functions as a support group. A learning community may exist within an organization or across a number of different organizations. Members may be located within a building, across a country or across the world.

The growth of virtual learning communities

Virtual learning communities provide an opportunity for individuals with a common purpose to come together across barriers in time and space. Virtual communities use a variety of online communication tools to support their interactions and these include e-mail, discussion boards and conferencing tools. This means that busy professionals and individuals who are geographically isolated from their peers can access a community of peers at a time and place that suits them. Many virtual learning communities also involve face-to-face meetings. It is important to note that many virtual learning communities do not carry out all their activities using technology. Many communities combine a range of approaches including online, face-to-face, facilitator-led and resource-based activities. This 'blended learning' approach provides many communities with an effective environment for learning. Data gathered from research into learning communities has shown that the participants rate a blended learning approach more highly than 'pure' online communications. Our own research supports this evidence. Most of the virtual learning communities referred to in this book are communities that have adopted a blended learning approach and very few of our examples refer to exclusively online communities.

Virtual learning communities have arisen during the last decade as a response to a variety of drivers and these include:

- intensifying competition and globalization;
- new ways of working, for example collaborative partnerships;
- accelerating change and the need to manage change and problem solve;
- the information explosion and the rise of knowledge management;
- developing and converging communication and information technologies;
- the need for continuous professional development.

In response to an increasingly complex and uncertain world, individuals have begun to connect and work together through online communities. Globalization and the need for economies to compete in world markets is driving a current collaboration agenda. In Britain, many government initiatives and funding streams demand evidence of collaborative partnership working and the better use and integration of services and resources. Collaboration provides a means through which representatives from different organizations and sectors can develop an understanding and appreciation of each other's perspectives. Increasingly multi-professional groups are brought together to develop strategic responses to sector-specific problems, for example the NHS Teaching Trusts are bringing together health services, social services, police services, education, and library services; the UK government's SureStart initiative brings together a diverse range of professionals including social workers, healthcare workers, librarians, nursery nurses and play specialists. Learning communities often develop within these collaborative initiatives or as a by-product of them.

The rise of globalization and the practice of working across national boundaries and continents is also shifting individual workers towards new ways of working and communicating. Workers within the same organization may be located in 20 or more countries and need to work together in virtual teams that only meet face-to-face at irregular intervals, if at all. The development of learning technologies and online communities enables these workers to 'meet together' and share their knowledge and expertise, and develop as virtual learning communities.

Accelerated change is an inevitable consequence of globalization and advances in communication and information technologies. Accelerated change requires increasingly smart ways of working which are likely to involve both product and process innovation. Nowadays the majority of professional workers are very familiar with increased rates and types of change. Working with and, possibly, moving to the forefront of change requires knowledge and skills in managing change, managing oneself (stress management, time management), managing uncertainty, managing multiple projects, and developing learning in organizations and their teams. One response to coping with the demands of accelerated change has led to the development of virtual learning communities to enable individuals to work in a supportive environment on real workplace issues at a time and place that suits their work–life balance.

Ward (1999) states:

> The information explosion continues in size, complexity and diversity. Information overload is a recognized stress stimulus and our business is in managing, organizing and enabling the exploitation of information, so that we have control and contain the explosion on behalf of organisations and individuals who need or demand not overload but filtered, validated and authoritative information.

The continuing information explosion demands that individuals develop effective approaches to managing information and learning communities can help individuals to deal with information overload by sharing information and helping each other to evaluate and engage in the process of information assimilation by filtering out unnecessary information.

The convergence of accelerated change, information explosion, and communication technologies has resulted in the development of knowledge management practices within organizations. Knowledge management practices focus on knowledge as an organization's key asset and work towards identifying the knowledge of individuals and teams so that this can be used effectively and made available to the whole organization. Knowledge management practices also aim to foster processes like knowledge creation, transfer, application and evolution in order to create value within an organization. A common approach to managing knowledge within organizations is to differentiate between explicit and tacit knowledge. Nonaka (1991) says:

> Explicit knowledge is formal and systematic. For this reason it can be easily communicated and shared, in product specifications or a scientific formula or a computer program. Tacit knowledge is highly personal. It is hard to formalise and therefore difficult, if not impossible, to communicate.

In many respects learning communities are concerned with explicit knowledge and also the codification of tacit knowledge into explicit knowledge. The process of transforming tacit into explicit knowledge is a key activity of learning communities. Community participants explore experience and practice, interrogate new ideas, concepts and evidence, discuss personal perspectives and concerns with fellow professional workers and such interactions often result in the development of clarity and a shared language. This process, particularly in a virtual community, often leads to the development and capture of previously tacit professional knowledge and practice as explicit knowledge and skills. Learning communities also provide a vehicle whereby new members, for example newly qualified professionals, are able to tap into the tacit and explicit knowledge of experienced practitioners.

Corrall (1999) differentiates between three different approaches to managing knowledge:

- **Databases and repositories** are commonly used for managing explicit knowledge and they are used for storing information and documents, for example reports, marketing materials, project documents, minutes of meetings, training materials, manuals, handbooks, etc.
- **Knowledge route maps and directories** are used to guide people to: individuals with specific expertise, skills or experience; specialist datasets and document collections. These are therefore concerned with explicit and tacit knowledge.
- **Knowledge communities and networks** provide opportunities for individuals to come together in learning communities, communities of practice or communities of interest. These offer important opportunities whereby tacit knowledge can be captured, shared, explored and harvested.

Yogesh Malhortra (2004) argues that many knowledge-management systems fail because organizations place too much emphasis on the first two approaches, that is databases and knowledge route maps; he says that organizations focus on getting the right knowledge to the right person at the right time. This approach works well in predictable and stable environments with a primary focus on knowledge harvesting and reuse and replication. However, he argues in the unpredictable business environments that many organizations now face, knowledge is, in fact, a dynamic construct and diverse meanings are possible based on diverse interpretations of the same information inputs across different contexts and at different times. What is done with data information and best practices depends on the subjective interpretation of the individuals and groups transforming information into actions and performance. He argues that too many organizations rely on databases, web-based information repositories and information directories and that the only effective way to manage knowledge in the twenty-first century is to develop systems that rely on the human interpretation of information. If the purpose of knowledge management is to transform information into human actions and performance then work-based learning communities have an important role to play. One advantage of virtual learning communities is that they provide written evidence of the knowledge development process and this is then accessible to the whole community and the sponsoring organization.

The convergence of information and communications technologies has resulted in new developments in communication technology designed to extend the possibilities for individuals to communicate with each other. Commonly used tools include: conferencing software, low-cost video conferencing, group communications software, virtual learning environments (VLEs) and advanced information retrieval software. These technologies are making an impact on both individuals and the ways in which we work, learn and collaborate with each other. This in turn is impacting on our working environments. As a result the world of work (public and private sector) is now often characterized by:

- new and simpler organizational structures;
- blurred boundaries – within and between organizations, within and between traditional professional groups;
- rise in cooperative and collaborative partnerships;
- complex organizational relationships;
- 24/7 working;
- free and extremely fast exchange of information between individuals and communities across the globe;
- new approaches to work, for example virtual teams, virtual learning communities;
- new approaches to staff development, for example replacement of traditional training programmes with a blended mix of face-to-face and online activities;
- increasing concerns about data protection, privacy, confidentiality.

Benefits of virtual learning communities

Membership and involvement in virtual learning communities bring a range of benefits to individuals, organizations, and sectors, bringing partners together across the wider professions. These are outlined and discussed below.

Individuals

The benefits of membership of virtual learning communities have already been touched on but are perhaps best illustrated through the statements of those who have experienced the transforming and dynamic power of learning communities, for example:

I was unsure what to expect when my manager suggested that I joined the company project learning community. Members of the community were physically located around the company in different departments and sites. At first I felt shy and uncomfortable about 'chatting' online. It improved when I had a real problem with my marketing project. I posted a message to the community and immediately got some helpful replies. A guy in Scotland has experienced the same problem and he phoned me up. We talked it through and worked out what to do next. To my surprise he thanked me for my query and said that he'd learnt something new from the discussion too. After this I felt OK and more involved in the community. It's a great way to share knowledge and skills. It means that staff throughout the whole country are working together even if we never see each other. When I applied for promotion I asked the community for help and got lots of useful advice and guidance on what the panel might be looking for. It meant that I went into the interview feeling really confident. I got the job! We shared a virtual glass of champagne online. One important point is that everything is confidential – no one else can read our messages.

Steve, Engineering Company

Sam, an NHS Training Manager, gave the following feedback at the end of a 'blended' learning community training programme.

I enjoyed the experience of participating in a new way of working and learning. I liked the flexibility and autonomy of being able to participate and grapple with the training when I can fit it in rather than being ruled by meetings/group time. It was OK not having to work face-to-face with the group but still learning and sharing experiences relevant to the training . . . I really enjoyed being a participant. I found the facilitator support very helpful and the feedback timely and constructive. I will definitely consider the potential of forming learning communities when tackling training issues and projects that require collaboration in the future. I think there is great scope for developing learning communities within the NHS.

Sam, NHS Training Manager

Some of the benefits individuals have cited in our evaluations of communities are listed in Box 1.1.

Box 1.1   Benefits of membership of a VLC

- Access to information and expertise at a time and place to suit me
- Access to like-minded individuals
- Access to mutual support
- Opportunities to collaborate with and learn from others
- Shared perspectives
- Opportunities to interrogate data and theory with input from others
- Dynamic new approaches to learning
- Working 'out-of-the-box' more creativity
- Opportunities to try out new ideas
- Empowered to challenge accepted institution/organization assumptions
- Opportunity to find innovative solutions to complex problems
- Sense of identity and group membership
- Support and friendship
- Opportunity to 'let off steam' in a safe environment
- Improved group outputs
- Collective responsibilities
- Confidence building

We have found that learning communities are particularly helpful for the following groups of professionals:

1   New entrants to a profession who are managing the challenges of establishing their own professional credibility. Learning communities provide incipient professionals with ready access to established practitioners' knowledge and experience, offering a safe environment in which to model and observe professional practice, and build and develop professional knowledge and understanding.
2   Individuals who are moving into situations that are new to them, for example as a result of a change in employment in which they want quickly to develop relevant knowledge and expertise.
3   Individuals who are working at the forefront of specialist knowledge and tackling new problems and unique situations. VLCs provide them with access to experienced colleagues with whom they can discuss and construct knowledge and develop new approaches to practice.
4   Individuals/teams who are required to implement strategic changes within an organization or region transcending traditional boundaries.
5   Those with a strategic responsibility for workforce development.

In our experience, the potential of learning communities to provide an effective route to continuing professional development (CPD) has not yet been fully exploited. As professional organizations and agencies increasingly promote and require evidence of individuals' CPD activity, it is likely that the potential of learning communities will be utilized further. The past decade has seen professional associations move towards increasingly high standards for CPD. For example, the Royal College of Physicians has recently approved new standards for CPD and these include:

- CPD is a requirement for all members and Fellows with responsibilities in the faculty.
- CPD is an essential component of revalidation for all doctors practising as specialists.
- CPD is open to public health professionals from other disciplines. The system is based on multi-professional public health practice.
- The new system allows CPD to be recorded through credits that encompass a broad range of activities in public health practice.
- Achievement of a minimum of 50 credits every year is obligatory.

Professional standards such as these clearly identify the potential of learning communities to provide dynamic new modes for supporting multi-professional collaborative approaches to CPD. Learning communities provide a forum for sharing good practice, collaborative problem solving and expanding skills and expertise, and such networks enable individuals to keep up to date. In addition it is easy to evidence active membership of such a community as virtual activities leave a paper trail. Membership of learning communities may also lead to enhanced professional reputation and so increased marketability and employability. A checklist of benefits is shown in Box 1.2.

Box 1.2   Checklist of benefits of virtual learning communities to support CPD activity

- Encourages professional knowledge sharing and knowledge management
- Helps specialists assigned to individual project teams connect with specialists in other organizations in other geographical locations
- Encourages multi-professional working
- Virtual place to discuss issues related to effective daily practices; improved productivity and services; and enables community members to work more efficiently at lower cost
- Encourages cross-sector collaboration
- Online discussions automatically recorded and evidenced
- Experts can be brought in to give inputs on specific themes
- Provides flexibility in time, pace and place
- Opportunities for acquiring new knowledge
- Gives practitioners more effective ways to address problems or current issues
- Challenges people to be more creative
- Promotes leadership and peer support
- Collaborative activities promote new techniques

Organizations

Nickols (2000) outlines the business case for virtual learning communities as 'for a quite modest investment in today's resources, organisations can reap huge rewards in terms of tomorrow's results'. Our experiences of working in learning communities within a number of sectors, for example manufacturing, health and education, demonstrate that the organizational benefits included better team working, creative approach to problem solving, greater understanding of practices and issues experienced in different departments, sharing of good practice, increased motivation, improved team working and reduction in sense of isolation. Box 1.3 shows a checklist of benefits for organizations.

Across a sector

While learning communities often exist within an organization where their work may be focused on enabling individuals and teams to share and construct knowledge and solve business problems, they also exist across

---

Box 1.3   Checklist of benefits for organizations

- Shared information and expertise
- Team building
- Knowledge management
- Development of good practice
- Empowered to challenge accepted institutional assumptions
- Opportunity to find innovative solutions to complex problems
- Enhanced sense of identity and group membership
- Effective working across traditional departmental boundaries
- Improved communication
- More highly motivated staff
- Positive impact on staff morale
- Develops a culture of change and innovation
- Dynamic problem solving and 'out-of-the-box' solutions
- Development of learning organizational practices
- Continuing professional development of those involved
- Increased productivity
- Increased levels of practitioner competence
- Service improvements

---

organizations. This type of learning community may be supported by a professional or trade organization or by regional strategic partnerships, and their purpose may be:

- dissemination of good practice;
- innovation and improved practices;
- to provide opportunities for international collaboration;
- multi-professional collaboration; and
- cross-sector collaboration to improve performance.

Examples of this type of VLC include Nurse2Nurse (described in Chapter 2), and Talking Heads.

Talking Heads
Talking Heads is an online community of head teachers that was supported by the DfES and the National College of School Leadership. It came online in November 2000 and it provides a wide range of opportunities for head teachers to talk with each other and to share best practice, debate current issues and problem solve. In addition it helps to overcome the isolation that many head teachers feel. The project employs a number of facilitators whose role includes seeding the site with relevant information, helping to initiate and establish conversations, providing technical support, and helping individuals to network. The software used for the site is think.com and this evolved through a collaborative partnership between Ultralab and Oracle.

Within Talking Heads itself there are different types of community including communities of interest, that is large communities of 3000+ members which provide open access to general resources and discussion groups; small special interest communities focused on specific issues; and also local working groups which are often an online extension of an existing local community. Evaluation of Talking Heads identifies the value of this online community, for example in response to the question 'Is participating in Talking Heads increasing your effectiveness as a head teacher?'; 82 per cent of heads from the first-year pilot replied 'yes'. Examples of how it increased their effectiveness included:

'Getting information about performance management, from both the horse's mouth and from other heads.'

'Debating new initiatives and gaining a greater understanding of the implications from fellow heads has enabled me to implement some policies more effectively, by being aware of some of the pitfalls others have faced.'

'I got some good advice on-line regarding a tricky parent, plus felt that I was less isolated and that at least someone else could understand the dilemma.'

'I can find things out easily and without thinking it's something I should already know. There are some things you just don't ask county advisors for fear of appearing inadequate.'

'The contact with other people who face similar challenges has been very helpful, but more importantly, I can "benchmark" my ideas against the opinions of other professionals, and so have a relative measure of how I am doing.'

(Jones *et al.* 2000)

Summary

This chapter introduces the concept of learning communities and virtual learning communities and describes the scope and context of the book. Learning communities provide an important way in which individuals come together to work on work-related problems and issues, develop new knowledge and skills, and improve performance in the workplace. In this book, the term 'learning community' is used loosely to include learning programmes, learning communities and communities of practice. Virtual learning communities are those that make use of online communication tools such as e-mail, discussion groups and chat rooms, and they provide a way in which individuals can work and learn together either within or across organizational or geographic boundaries. Members of many virtual learning communities also meet up face-to-face and this blended approach is one that is taken in many of the case studies and examples discussed in the book. Finally, the benefits of virtual learning communities are considered with reference to individuals, organizations and the wider professional context.

2

Models of Learning Communities

Introduction

This chapter provides an overview of three models of learning communities and their working practices. These models were developed in response to the needs of a range of organizations, from those wanting to introduce a virtual learning community as part of a learning programme through to those wanting to implement a strategic change which utilized online communities as a means of enabling the change to take place. In this chapter each of these models is illustrated with examples from practice. Learning communities may be self-organizing or sponsored by an organization or strategic partnerships; some have facilitators while others are free-flowing; some involve face-to-face meetings while others exist entirely online. Examples of these different working practices are discussed with respect to actual community examples.

Different types of virtual learning communities

Virtual learning communities are normally set up for a specific purpose such as to support workforce development, to provide a means through which problems and issues may be tackled, or to support team working and learning in an innovative way. VLCs are established for a variety of reasons including:

- as a strategic response to an identified need for workforce development either within an organization or within an economic region;
- to encourage multi-professional integrated responses to complex situations;
- to enable workers to overcome geographical boundaries in time and space;

- to support continuous professional development;
- to cascade new work practices through organizations;
- to bring people together to share good practice;
- to provide new approaches to learning or service improvements;
- to support learning and training programmes;
- to achieve project outputs.

In addition they may develop spontaneously as a response to work-based problems and issues. The purpose and location of a learning community defines the type of community that is formed. They may be found within one organization, working across a number of organizations, or across a sector or across national and international boundaries. They may be entirely self-contained or alternatively supported through a set of formal links involving a strategic management group, ICT support and other organizational functions. The following models were developed in response to the needs of practitioners and this section will introduce their structure and discuss them with reference to examples from practice. There are three basic models of VLCs and these are discussed in turn:

- the simple learning community;
- the managed learning community; and
- the complex learning community.

Simple virtual learning community

In this type of example the community often forms spontaneously as members (who may or may not be employed by the same organization) come together and establish a community as a result of shared interests or common problems. Members may come from different departments and units within the organization, or across a number of organizations, or from one or many countries. There are four patterns of membership in simple VLCs:

- Small core of active members. Closed group. Membership remains the same over time.
- Small core membership. Open group. Membership changes over time. Core of active members.
- Large membership. Closed group. Small changes in membership over time.
- Large membership. Open group. Relatively large changes in membership over time. Core of active members who provide stability.

There may be a self-appointed facilitator, the community may select its own facilitator or the role of facilitator may be rotated (see Figure 2.1). In its relationship with employing organizations this type of community may exist (and often does) outside the everyday formal structures and supporting

Figure 2.1   Simple virtual learning community

mechanisms. In some cases this can lead to conflict between the members of the VLC and the organization.

University of Hull Blackboard group
Within the University of Hull there is an online community based around individuals' interests and use of the virtual learning environment Blackboard. This group communicates via an e-mail discussion list and members may meet up, for example for demonstrations, to share good practice, to lobby for improvements to the system, etc. The group is not formally facilitated, although the university's e-learning team take responsibility for organizing meetings and act as an official information channel between the group and the university central ICT services.

TLG group
Barbara Allan has been involved in a self-organizing VLC that arose out of a formal academic programme. This involved six college and university lecturers who came together in a virtual community to write a research article on their experiences as e-learners. The VLC existed for six months and culminated in members of the group meeting face-to-face at the conference where they presented their paper. In this virtual community members reported the following experiences:

> I've felt a greater sense of personal responsibility e.g. to other group members, and put a lot of time and care into reading messages/work and giving feedback.

> There was a good group ethos and I feel an honest exchange of ideas/criticisms happened at all times.

> I think all of my hopes have been achieved with the added bonus that we may have a paper to reflect our efforts and to be disseminated to a wider audience.

I think we were all honest, direct and stringent in our feedback and that there was a strong sense of cooperation and objectivity.

(Allan *et al.* 2002)

Once it had achieved its goal the group disbanded, although some members still keep in touch via e-mail. The evaluation of the TLG group indicated that members experienced the following advantages as a result of their experiences:

- a sense of increased motivation;
- excitement about doing something different;
- enthusiasm for researching the issue;
- freedom to pursue their own ideas;
- opportunities for developing new ways of autonomous working;
- opportunities for working with peers in new ways.

The main issues that arose from this experience related to the group having developed out of a formal academic programme and difficulties that arose in terms of re-integrating with the main group, and also some tensions between TLG group members and others in the main group. This example is explored in more detail in Allan *et al.* (2002).

What are the benefits and potential challenges in a simple learning community? The answers to the question are summarized in Table 2.1. In this type of community individual members will transfer their knowledge and skills developed within the community to their colleagues in the workplace, a reverse transfer will also take place. This is illustrated in Figure 2.2.

Table 2.1 Simple virtual learning community

Benefits of a simple learning community	*Potential issues*
Provides a meeting ground for like-minded individuals	Becomes a clique and undermines more formal structures and processes
Provides a way in which individuals can tackle common problems or issues	Works outside traditional boundaries and so does not link its work into organizational requirements
May cut across traditional structures and boundaries within the organization and so facilitate dissemination of information and good practice	Focus is on members' interests rather than organizational issues

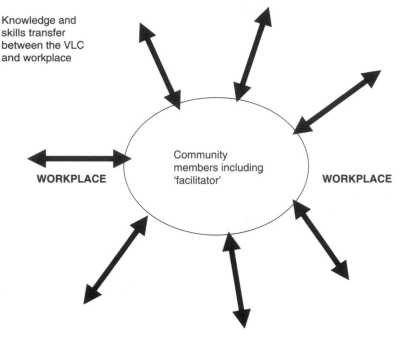

Knowledge and
skills transfer
between the VLC
and workplace

WORKPLACE

Community
members including
'facilitator'

WORKPLACE

Figure 2.2   Transfer of knowledge into the workplace in a simple virtual learning
community

Managed virtual learning community

Managed virtual learning communities are formally supported by an
organization or agency and community members and facilitator(s) may be
drawn from one or more organizations (see Figure 2.3). The community is
supported by a facilitator who reports to an appropriate management group.
This type of virtual learning community is often developed within one organization and in response to a strategic need, for example new problems, project work. In this model the management group is critical to the life of the
VLC as it identifies the need for a learning community, for example to deal
with a new project or issue. It then initiates and nurtures the community
until it is functioning independently; this process is likely to involve a
facilitator. Members of the learning community develop their professional
practice through participation in the learning community and then transfer
their new learning understanding and expertise into the workplace. This
process is likely to be monitored and managed by the management group.

Birmingham VLC
This learning community was established by the Birmingham University
Learning Development Unit as part of a strategic plan to develop staff

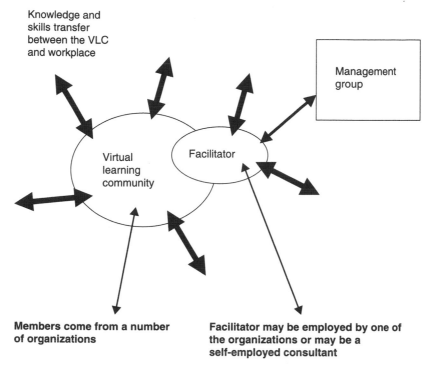

Knowledge and
skills transfer
between the VLC
and workplace

Management
group

Virtual
learning
community

Facilitator

**Members come from a number
of organizations**

**Facilitator may be employed by one of
the organizations or may be a
self-employed consultant**

Figure 2.3 Virtual learning community across a number of organizations

knowledge, skills and practice in e-learning. Two external facilitators facilitated the e-learning training programme during the first phase, then participants from the first programme facilitated the next phase and this resulted in the development and embedding of good practice in e-learning across the university.

The development of a managed VLC provides a number of benefits and potential challenges for organizations, as shown in Table 2.2.

The previous example considered a virtual learning community that was established by an individual employer. Virtual learning communities also offer an important means for professional development and may be sponsored by a professional group or a trade association. In addition online conferences, which may be considered as temporary communities, also offer an important route for the exchange of ideas and good practice, as illustrated in the following examples.

Nurse2Nurse
Nurse2Nurse provides an example of a community established by a professional association to enable their members to develop their knowledge and skills. This learning community was established by the Irish Nurses

Table 2.2 Managed virtual learning community

Benefits	Potential issues
Management group provides appropriate support, e.g. administrative and technical to the VLC	Members may be volunteers or conscripts
The learning community is clearly linked to and focused on organizational needs	Members may not be committed to the purpose of the learning community
External facilitators bring in new ideas and approaches	Members may not prioritize their membership of the community
Collaborative approaches to problem solving and fewer decisions made out of self-interest	Facilitators may not fully understand organizational cultures or priorities
Learning community may be made up of people from different organizations leading to multi-professional working practices	Stakeholders may want to get involved in the learning community
Leads to collaborative learning across traditional boundaries	Community members may go off and 'do their own thing'
Can break down barriers between organizations and sectors	Working with other professionals can be very challenging and tensions may develop
Can lead to dynamic new approaches to tackling institutionalized problems	Participants can feel exposed by contributing their ideas in the written word
Increases flexibility in communicating with colleagues: any time, any place asynchronous discussions	Work–life balance issues; need to be aware of potential for overwork

Association to provide an online community of practice where nurses could share good practice and discuss current issues or problems. The community is focused around a website (www.nurse2nurse.ie) which is maintained and updated by a librarian-facilitator who provides access to a wide range of health information sources as well as providing ICT training and support to the nurses. In this community the librarian-facilitator spent significant amounts of time ensuring that members had the appropriate ICT skills, access to the website and also helped to create the conditions to support a culture change towards using a VLC as a tool for professional development.

Short-lived VLC
One variation of the managed VLC exists in online conferences, which can be seen as short-lived or temporary learning communities. Virtual conferences are becoming increasingly common and important as a means of exchanging ideas and good practice. Unlike traditional face-to-face conferences that may only take place over a few days or a week, virtual conferences may last much

longer, for example a fortnight of scheduled events followed by two months of discussions by conference members. In this way they can be considered as temporary learning communities.

An example of a virtual conference is one that took place during 2003 on communities of practice and it was hosted through a specialist website (see http://www.icohere.com) which provides participants with access to a series of pre-conference sessions. The actual conference itself was made up of keynote presentations, papers and workshops all followed up through asynchronous and synchronous discussions (including a café) with follow-up access for two months after the close of the virtual event. A vast range of activities take place in the virtual conference sites and they may include: keynote presentations, for example by narrated PowerPoint slides or webcasts, asynchronous discussions and real-time chat sessions, Q and A sessions, a virtual café, syndicate rooms and breakout activities. Our experiences in taking part in these temporary VLCs are very positive, they provide direct contact with experts and like-minded people and sometimes the biggest challenge is working out the time zones! High-quality technical support and the availability of a virtual technical help desk is vital.

The benefits and potential issues for temporary VLCs are shown in Table 2.3.

Table 2.3 Temporary virtual learning communities

Benefits	*Potential issues*
Provides a meeting ground for like-minded individuals	Poor or no facilitation means that the community doesn't get started
Provides a way in which individuals can tackle common problems or issues	Becomes a clique
Facilitates dissemination of information and good practice	Community fizzles out if key members leave
Cuts across traditional boundaries, e.g. organizations, sectors	Conflicts of interest between participants' organizations and work roles
Doesn't involve expensive travel or time away from workplace	Industrial espionage and rivalry between organizations, e.g. in product development

Complex virtual learning community

Complex VLCs are often formed to achieve widespread improvements within organizations or geographical regions and they may involve a range of strategic affiliations and partnerships (see Figure 2.4). Those involved in the management of such groups often identify that their strategic aims could

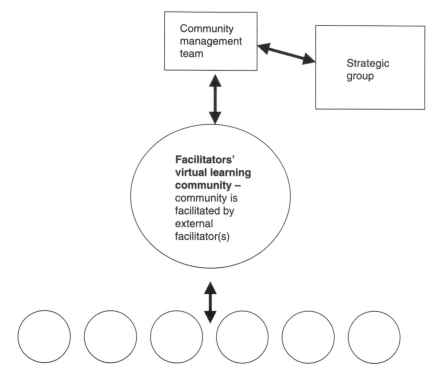

Figure 2.4   Complex virtual learning community

be achieved effectively through the formation of learning communities. Strategic partnerships often sponsor the formation of learning communities with a focus on workforce development. We have been involved in a range of strategic partnerships providing support and guidance on the pedagogy of virtual leaning communities. Typically, a community management group focuses on enabling the virtual learning communities to become operational and it includes staff from human resources departments, technical experts, administrators and community champions. External facilitators help to train and develop internal facilitators, who then facilitate the learning communities. In this type of example the strategic group is likely to provide detailed input at the foundation stage and it will then monitor the life of the community. It will take an active role in the evaluation of the community and its outputs.

This type of structure was established by the Northern Centre for Mental Health (NCMH) for a project we were involved in during the period from 2000 to 2002. The aim of the NCMH Project was to enable change within the NHS through the establishment of a series of learning communities each with its own facilitator. We were involved in training the facilitators. The training process took place through a series of face-to-face meetings and activities in an online e-learning group. Each facilitator then led their own learning community which focused on issues such as user and carer involvement, leadership for change, service development and redesign, and policy implementation. Some of the issues raised at the start of the process were problems of access to ICT and difficulties caused by the firewalls set up within the NHS ICT systems and those of the university. Initially it was anticipated that groups would comprise multi-professional teams but individuals opted to work within their own professional groups.

Complex virtual learning communities may also develop as a result of the establishment of successful simple or managed learning communities. This is illustrated in the following case study.

VLCs as a response to skills shortages
Greater Economic Success is the name given to the North Lincolnshire Strategic Partnership action group responsible for the strategic direction of the North Lincolnshire economy. The group involves over 20 of the area's largest manufacturers and meets every 6 to 8 weeks. The group identifies key issues that affect their business performance and attempt to find solutions. They believe that adding value to existing company processes will establish a more efficient base from which to grow the economy of North Lincolnshire. Issues addressed so far include: European Working Time Directive, strategic management, supply chain management, Health and Safety and Lean Manufacturing.

The University of Hull has worked successfully with the Greater Economic Success group in identifying, developing and accrediting 10 new short programmes to address training and skills gaps needs for managers in the region. One of the authors (Dina Lewis) established simple learning communities in companies with identified skills gaps and provided support and facilitated training sessions. Examples of these are the Lime Product Manufacturing Company and an industrial cleaning company servicing and located at a steel works in Scunthorpe.

Lime Product Manufacturing Company
The North Lincolnshire Strategic Partnership identified the need for strategic management training for key companies in the region. The entire senior management team including the managing director from a successful lime product manufacturing company signed up to participate in a training programme on strategic management skills. We worked with colleagues from the Kingsway Business Centre at North Lindsey College, Scunthorpe to provide the required management training by establishing a learning community. We co-facilitated face-to-face sessions, reviewing the organization's strategic plan, including their mission statement and key performance indicators. A virtual learning environment (VLE) was used as the central communications tool for the learning community, the discussion board was used

to record ongoing discussions and save time in face-to-face meetings, the VLE provided hyperlinks to their competitors' websites and professional organizations linked to their sector, and all our training materials were made available through the virtual learning environment. Evaluations revealed that the group thought that they had bonded more closely as a team and that their approach to tackling interdepartmental problems and issues had improved. Individuals were more prepared to consider the implications of their actions on other colleagues and departments, the programme had encouraged collaborative interdepartmental approaches to working and learning with a direct impact on the work practices of those involved.

Facilitating a learning community in the steel industry
This same partners also set up a programme to improve management practices within a service company located at a steel works and this involved working with a group of operations managers. The company identified the need to improve management practices and we worked to establish a learning community with a focus on that specific area. This was a small pilot project and limited to six middle managers from the company. They met for regular facilitated face-to-face action learning/training sessions, focusing on different areas of management skills. In addition, the managers communicated with us and also each other using virtual communication tools such as a bulletin board and chat room. This enabled them to keep their discussions flowing in between the face-to-face sessions, as they worked on different shifts on sites in two UK cities. Although this community was supported by the company and established by us as part of an accredited learning programme, individual members took responsibility for the virtual communication and used the VLE to problem solve and stimulate debate on topics not covered during the formal training sessions. Achievements by the group included improving health and safety practices, improving induction training, and improving management information systems and recruitment and selection practices. These topics were not covered during the facilitated workshop sessions, we did however consider continuous improvement practices and the participants were highly motivated and proactive and used their initiative to transfer their learning from the programme to improve work-based practices in a wide range of areas.

These are both examples of managed virtual learning communities and this experience and their success led us to identify the need for a more strategic approach to supporting the establishment of learning communities in the North Lincolnshire region. As a result there is a proposal to bring together all 20 partner companies already committed to the North Lincolnshire Strategic Partnership to support a virtual learning community approach to improving knowledge transfer and higher level skills in the region. The identified benefits of using virtual learning communities as a tool for workforce strategic development include:

- Improved communications between the 20 companies involved.
- Better collaboration between organizations, sharing of current and best practice.
- The identification of issues specific to the region.
- Exciting opportunities to share and transfer knowledge and experience.
- Access to a wide range of central and national online resources.
- Knowledge construction and knowledge management.
- Changes in work practices across organizations.
- Virtual visits from experts in the field.
- Sustained growth and development of the GES group.
- Competitive advantage for the region.

Supporting the NHS North and East Yorkshire and North Lincolnshire
Workforce Development Confederation (WDC) e-Learning strategy
Another example of the use of VLCs as a tool for implementing strategic change and also cascading knowledge and skills within an organization is found in the WDC e-Learning strategy. The WDC, as the organization funding training within the NHS, approached the Centre for Lifelong Learning at the University of Hull to discuss the potential for developing virtual learning communities throughout the WDC region to support their implementation of an e-Learning strategy. The WDC's e-Learning strategy is focused on improving the use of learning technologies to support effective learning communities throughout the North and East Yorkshire and North Lincolnshire region. It was agreed that the university would work in partnership with the WDC via a three-phase programme to share knowledge and understanding of the underpinning pedagogies that support effective collaborative e-learning.

Phase one

The University of Hull programme director worked in partnership with three e-learning coordinators to adapt the 'Facilitating online learning communities' programme to meet the needs of staff within the NHS. The e-learning coordinators recruited a group of 16 trainers and training managers and e-learning champions within the NHS (this included the e-learning coordinators themselves). This programme has now taken place and utilized both face-to-face and online community activities using the university's Blackboard virtual learning environment. Participants were highly motivated and keen to develop skills in supporting online learning communities.

Phase two

Once the pilot group has completed the 'blended' training programme they will form pairs to co-deliver the training programme to other groups of participants using the university 10-credit module and learning materials. It is expected that eight learning communities will be formed and each learning community is likely to have 12 participants, so the expected numbers involved in the training during phase two are likely to be around 100. Phase two was scheduled to run in April 2004. The pilot group of trainers will work in pairs to co-facilitate new communities of new trainers. During this phase the university programme director will mentor the trainers, offer support and manage the university quality assurance mechanisms.

Phase three

In the third phase of implementation, trainers will establish learning communities, some of the trainers will continue to deliver the training in facilitating online learning communities, and other participants will go on to facilitate communities of practice addressing real service issues in the NHS. Thus cascading the knowledge and understanding of communities of practice throughout the organization.

This pilot project has been funded by the WDC, and the NHS University is following the development with interest. This programme provides an example of a complex learning community and it is one in which knowledge and skills will be cascaded through an organization.

Working practices

The previous section explores three different models of virtual learning communities and here we will focus on the different types of working practices that may be established within different communities. The working practices of learning communities vary according to the needs of the group members and examples include whether or not they are self-organizing or sponsored, the use of a facilitator or self-facilitated communities, the ways in which they meet (face-to-face, online, blended), their use of ICT, and also their life span.

Self-organizing and sponsored communities

A useful distinction to make is the difference between self-organizing and sponsored learning communities. Nickols (2000) describes self-organizing VLCs as frequently involving individuals coming together on a voluntary and informal basis. These communities may have evolved out of a project, conference or e-mail discussion group and they enable individuals to follow their interests and develop their expertise or specialism. The TLG group discussed above (pp. 22–3) as an example of a simple virtual learning community arose spontaneously out of a two-year-long virtual learning community and it existed for about six months. This was a self-organizing community and different people within the community took on different roles, for example editor or progress chaser depending on their interests, skills and availability.

On the other hand, sponsored VLCs are initiated, organized and supported by employers, professional bodies or other agencies. They are established to produce specific outcomes of benefit to the sponsor. Many sponsored learning communities are facilitated, for example, by an internal or external experienced facilitator. All the examples of managed and complex VLCs given above are sponsored by the employer and, in some cases, by professional associations, for example Nurse2Nurse.

Facilitated and free-flowing

Learning communities may be facilitated or they may be free-flowing. Facilitated communities are often established within organizations as a means of enabling members to work on particular issues or problems and also to improve working practices. The organization may provide or nominate a facilitator who may be a member of staff or an external facilitator. In contrast free-flowing communities are not facilitated and their activities are spontaneous and determined entirely by their members.

Birmingham e-learning community and Nurse2Nurse
In both of these examples (see earlier in this chapter) the VLCs are facilitated. In the Birmingham e-learning example the university employed two external facilitators and this also provided a means of introducing new knowledge and skills into the community. In the Nurse2Nurse example the professional association employed someone who took on the role of information and knowledge manager as well as community facilitator.

Lighthouse Project Group
The Lighthouse Project Group was established in 2000 with the aim of providing independent trainers with a forum for improving their professional practice. It is a cooperative and membership is by invitation. It is a free-flowing community and, while one member takes responsibility for administering the website, there is no facilitator. The Lighthouse Project Group provides members with: an informal network of like-minded trainers and development workers; information, support, advice and learning resources; opportunities for sharing work; opportunities for personal and professional development. The Lighthouse Project Group is based around a website that provides an extensive range of ICT facilities.

The role of facilitator is an important one and it is explored in much more detail in Chapters 4 to 6. At this stage it is worth highlighting that the role of facilitator is just that, it is to facilitate the group rather than to act as a didactic leader, and in the context of learning communities the facilitator is often described as being a 'guide on the side'. The facilitator is likely to undertake the following types of roles and activities: consultant, guide, and resource provider; expert questioner; designer of learning experiences; community member; and to share control and power with other members.

Type of contact

Learning communities may involve a wide range of activities that include face-to-face meetings and/or online activities. Learning communities that involve their members in both face-to-face and online activities are sometimes said to take a 'blended' approach to their work. The majority of examples used in this book are blended and the communities meet face-to-face as well as benefit from online communications.

The advantages of a blended approach are that they provide the potential benefits of both face-to-face and virtual activities. Meetings and workshops are an extremely productive way of establishing a community, providing induction (including training in the use of ICT) and also carrying out a wide variety of activities. They provide the opportunity for members to match faces to names and to spend time socializing and getting to know each other. However, individuals who miss a meeting may feel that the group has moved on without them. In many situations it is physically impossible for members to get together. In contrast, online communications provide a means by which members can engage with each other and discuss and explore ideas in some depth at a time and place that suits them. However, the lack of visual cues such as body language can be a deterrent for some people.

Use of ICT

The use of ICT varies enormously and will range from a limited use of e-mail, for example to arrange face-to-face meetings and also to hold detailed discussions, to the use of sophisticated group communications and conferencing software or virtual learning environments. The use of different types of ICT by learning communities is explored in Chapter 3.

Life span

Learning communities may have a varied life span. In this book we are primarily concerned with communities that are likely to exist over a significant time period, for example one or two years. In contrast, the rise of online conferences means that some communities may come together for a relatively short time period.

Summary

This chapter has focused on three different models of VLC (simple, managed and complex) and these have been described with reference to practice. In reality, a wider range of VLCs exists and networks of VLCs may contain examples of each of the different models. Whatever the overall structure of the VLC it will be characterized by its working practices and these establish whether or not it is: self-organizing or sponsored by an organization or strategic partnerships; facilitated or free-flowing; face-to-face; entirely online or blended (a mixture of face-to-face and online); and govern its use of ICT and its life span. The next chapter will explore the use of ICT by virtual learning communities in some detail.

3

Virtual Communication Tools and Meeting Environments

Introduction

The aim of this chapter is to introduce the reader to a range of commonly used virtual communication tools. It is important that facilitators of virtual learning communities understand the range of online communication tools that are currently available as this will help them to select and use the tools that are most appropriate for their particular community. It is worth emphasizing that facilitators do not need specialist ICT skills as the majority of communication tools and virtual meeting environments are easy to set up and use.

Introduction to virtual communication tools

There are two main types of virtual communication tools and these enable different types of contacts between community members and facilitators:

- **Asynchronous tools** – enable people to communicate at a time that suits them. Individuals post a message that is held by the system. This message can be read and responded to as and when the recipient comes online. Asynchronous communications take place over time rather than at the same time. Examples of asynchronous tools commonly used in virtual learning communities include e-mail, bulletin boards and mailing lists.
- **Synchronous tools** – enable people to communicate when they log onto the same system at the same time, that is they are immediate and live communications. Unlike face-to-face communications a transcript or record of the communication process is provided by many synchronous tools. Examples of synchronous tools commonly used by virtual learning communities include conference or chat rooms, instant messaging, internet telephony and video conferencing.

Table 3.1 briefly describes these tools and gives examples of their application for virtual learning communities.

Table 3.1 Characteristics of virtual communication tools

	Type of communication	*Asynchronous/ synchronous*	*Virtual learning community applications*
E-mail	1 to 1, 1 to many	Asynchronous	Exchange information Provide detailed instruction Discussion Collaborative or project work Knowledge construction Training delivery, e.g. use of e-mail Follow-up coaching or mentoring sessions Network
Mailing lists	1 to many	Asynchronous	Exchange information Provide detailed instruction Discussion Collaborative or project work Knowledge construction Network
Bulletin boards	1 to many	Asynchronous	Exchange information Provide detailed instruction Discussions Collaborative or project work Knowledge construction Follow-up, e.g. coaching or mentoring sessions
Polling	1 to many	Asynchronous	Collect information Decision making
Instant messaging	1 to 1, 1 to many	Synchronous	Exchange information Provide detailed instruction Discussion Knowledge construction
Chat or conferencing	1 to 1, 1 to many	Synchronous	Exchange information Provide detailed instruction Discussions Collaborative or project work Knowledge construction Follow-up, e.g. coaching or mentoring sessions
Internet telephony	1 to 1, 1 to a few	Synchronous	Exchange information Provide detailed instruction Discussions Knowledge construction Training events, meetings
Video conferencing	1 to 1, 1 to a few	Synchronous	Exchange information Provide detailed instruction Discussions Knowledge construction Training events, meetings

E-mail

E-mail is such a widespread and common tool that it is often overlooked as a vehicle for group communications in a virtual learning community. Informal e-mail communication between individual practitioners where information and ideas are exchanged is possibly one of the most popular means of keeping up-to-date and solving small queries that arise every day in the workplace. E-mail is sometimes used as the underpinning communication tool for a virtual learning community and it offers a quick and familiar way in which community members can keep in touch with each other. Many practitioners find it more convenient to keep in touch with their learning community via e-mail rather than have to access a special website or virtual communications tool. In addition, sub-groups within a community may regularly use e-mail to keep in touch with each other and hold 'private' conversations.

Discussion or mail lists

There are thousands of discussion lists available on the internet and each is devoted to a particular topic and is aimed at a specific audience. Individual members may post an e-mail to the discussion list and this is immediately sent out via e-mail to all the list subscribers. They provide a quick and easy method of communication and often have a very speedy response time – sometimes within minutes! They are a good method of keeping up to date and also tapping into practical experience and expertise. The vast majority of discussion lists are open to anyone who wants to subscribe and they may have a membership of thousands, that is they are used by communities of interest rather than virtual learning communities or communities of practice.

Discussion or mail lists may also be closed to a specific group of people and access to the group is limited, they may be used by a virtual learning community as a means of communicating between group members. One of the advantages of using a discussion list compared with traditional e-mail is that membership is centralized and individual members need not update their address book each time someone enters or leaves the community. A facilitator of a virtual learning community who wants to set up a closed discussion list will find that they will be able to set one up by visiting sites such as: http://www.jiscmail.ac.uk. As with e-mail, members of virtual learning communities often find closed discussion groups an easy way of keeping in touch with each other as it means their messages are accessible via their e-mail system rather than needing to enter a special site.

Bulletin boards

Bulletin or discussion boards provide an asynchronous message forum and messages sent to a discussion group are permanently visible to everyone who

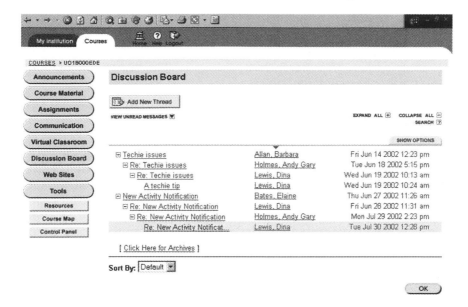

Figure 3.1 Example discussion board

has access to it. Many organizations and professional groups provide bulletin boards within their websites as a means of enabling their staff to discuss ideas and share information (see Figure 3.1).

A wide range of software packages enable the use of bulletin boards within websites. Sometimes online registration is required before you can access a bulletin board. A typical bulletin board provides the following features:

- indexes;
- basic search facility, for example by topic, author, keywords;
- tools to enable you to view bulletins in a hierarchical format, this is often called threaded or unthreaded where they are sorted by date/time;
- facilities to enable messages to be selected, saved and downloaded;
- facilities to indicate whether or not the user has read a particular message, for example red flags for unread messages.

Many virtual learning communities have access to closed bulletin boards and these enable individual members to have confidential access to the community. These bulletin boards may be hosted on an organization's website or intranet, alternatively they may be accessible via a virtual learning environment or group communication software. These are explored in more detail later in this chapter.

Polling software

Polling software enables a community facilitator to collect information from the whole group. It is particularly useful for identifying the optimum times(s) for online conferences.

Instant messaging

Instant messaging enables you to send and display a message on someone's screen in a matter of seconds. Instant message systems often have friend or buddy lists that enable individuals to track when one of the people on their list comes online so that they know the instant when they can start messaging them. This facility may be used by a virtual learning community. Examples of instant messaging software include ICQ ('I seek you') available from http://www.icq.com and AOL Instant Messenger available from http://www.newaol.com/aim.

Chat or conference software

Chat or conference software enables people to hold a 'live' discussion by sending each other short written messages. Chat software may be used to support individuals, provide quick advice and guidance to a member of staff, or as a coaching or mentoring tool. Chat software normally enables public and/or private conversations to take place and, depending on the software, these may be with individuals or groups.

Chatting online has a number of advantages as it can save time taken to travel and attend meetings, in addition the short telegraphic messages used in chat tend to result in short, concise meetings! The transcript of the session may be saved for future reference or research purposes. Chatting online is particularly helpful for people with hearing or speech impairments. As with most tools, there are disadvantages to online chat and these include the absence of non-verbal signals and the need to spend time becoming comfortable with online chat or conferencing.

Chat or conferencing facilities are often used by virtual learning communities and they are available in virtual learning environments and group communications software, which are explored later in this chapter.

Internet telephony

Synchronous communications now include internet telephony, which is the ability to make phone calls via the internet. These may be 1-to-1 calls or group calls. The advantage of internet telephony is that it enables individuals to make long-distance phone calls through the computer and the internet without paying expensive long-distance phone charges. However, it requires relatively up-to-date computers with access to a fast modem and large RAM, otherwise the sound quality may be poor.

Individuals using the internet for phone calls need to obtain a microphone for the computer and also to install internet telephone software. Increasingly organizations are combining internet telephony, e-mail, traditional phones, voice mail, and facsimile transmissions into powerful new unified messaging services.

Video conferencing

Video conferencing has been available for years but previously required specialist and very expensive equipment installed in specialist rooms. In recent years video conferencing packages have been developed for use on standard desktop computers. The use of desktop video conferencing is becoming more common and it offers a way in which members of the virtual learning community can 'come together' relatively easily.

Group communications software

There are now many different ways in which virtual communication tools can be made accessible to virtual learning communities, and this section explores two distinct approaches: commercial and non-commercial groupware.

Commercial groupware

Many organizations now use commercial communications software packages that offer a mix of e-mail, messaging, bulletin board and conference room facilities. Many of these packages also offer:

- A knowledge-management facility, for example through the use of document file systems with built-in content indexing and search to help users find and share information quickly.
- A basic project-management system, for example task management including scheduling, to do lists and automatic reminders.
- Data and video conferencing including real-time conferencing, document authoring, white boarding, text discussion and file transfer.

A common example is Lotus Notes; this integrates e-mail and business software for the internet and also corporate intranets. Lotus Notes provides a range of facilities including: e-mail, calendaring, group scheduling and a to do list. Integration with the Lotus Domino R5 Server makes Notes R5 a powerful communications tool enabling organizations to use a range of facilities from standards-based messaging to built-in collaborative applications like discussions and document libraries. Because Lotus Notes can be used with other business software it means that it can be used to create integrated learning environments within companies and other organizations. One advantage of this approach is that it means employees are familiar with these electronic tools and use them as an everyday part of their work, and so when they use them for virtual learning community applications this isn't viewed as a separate activity requiring a need to learn and use specialized software.

Virtual learning community using Lotus Notes
A group of information workers in the financial sector set up a virtual learning community to explore ways in which they could improve their units' internet searching training programmes. The group originally met on a day's training course in London, found that they had a lot in common, and as a result decided to set up a virtual learning community using a common tool, Lotus Notes. The virtual learning community was used as a vehicle for developing and testing new courses, obtaining feedback on training materials, and also sharing and identifying solutions to practical problems they encountered during their training programmes. Virtual learning community members worked together using Lotus Notes for about six months and then formally closed the community as they began to move forward in different directions. During the time that the virtual learning community existed it provided a valuable forum for learning and development.

Another example of this type of system is Microsoft Exchange 2000 and this offers an infrastructure for messaging, bulletin boards or discussion groups, contact and task management, and document management. It has built-in content indexing and search facilities to help users find and share information quickly. It also enables data and video conferencing including real-time conferencing, document authoring, white boarding, text discussion and file transfer. One of the real strengths of the system is that it provides management tools, for example the Conference Management Service keeps track of scheduled conferences and provides administrators with control of attendee access to conferences. Another strength is that information in Exchange 2000 can be accessed using Office 2000, web browsers, Microsoft Windows Explorer, cellular phones and handheld computers. This means it is accessible to virtual learning community facilitators and members in the workplace, at home and also on the move. This type of system was designed for large-scale use within organizations and it offers an alternative to large-scale virtual learning environments, which are discussed later in this chapter.

Another example of conferencing software is a groupware collaboration software platform called iCohere that can be integrated into the parent organization's existing site or used as a stand-alone collaborative platform. iCohere is also used to support virtual conferences, that is temporary learning communities. Everything is managed through simple templates using a standard web browser so that system administrators do not need specialist technical knowledge to manage the site. It provides virtual communities with an extensive range of facilities including:

- announcements
- shared documents and extensive document-managing system
- real-time instant messaging
- real-time group meetings
  - customized databases
  - integration of streaming PowerPoint files and other media
  - contact information including photographs
  - website links
  - security features.

iCohere is an extremely user-friendly interface with helpful and unobtrusive use of colour and icons, for example in the discussion board it is possible to mark your personal responses as shown in the following examples:

- Yes, I agree (accompanied by a thumbs-up sign).
- Next steps . . . (accompanied by some steps).
- I have a different perspective (accompanied by a pair of glasses).
- Here's a new twist (accompanied by a spiral shape with an arrow).
- Here's a resource (accompanied by a book).

More information on iCohere is available at http://www.icohere.com.

Non-commercial groupware

A growing number of groups and organizations provide access to integrated communication or learning environments and these often provide many of the facilities that are offered by the virtual learning environments or commercial group software packages. Access to this free or low-cost resource is important as it enables virtual learning communities to be formed in a diverse range of situations, for example the voluntary sector, independent practitioners, alternative health practitioners. With non-commercial groupware the host organization provides and maintains the technical facility and individuals or groups have access to their technical resources. Examples include www.intranets.com and www.quickteam.com. The advantages and disadvantages of a system such as www.intranets.com is explored in Table 3.2 and an example case study based on the use of this software is 'The Lighthouse Project Group' (see Chapter 2).

Using these systems is relatively easy and it can take less than 15 minutes to create this type of meeting environment. All that is required is that an individual takes out a subscription (often available for free for 30 days) and they are then provided with access to a named site. One or more people within the group may have administrator rights and they can ensure that membership is established for the whole group. They will have access to the following types of features: administration tools, calendar, polling facility, document facility, discussion facility, instant messaging, internet links, and a help facility. These are briefly described and the advantages and disadvantages of using this approach are summarized in Table 3.2.

Table 3.2 Advantages and disadvantages of non-commercial groupware

Facilities	Advantages	Disadvantages
General points	Free, simple, easy to use Access to online help and support Available to anyone with internet access	As it is free users can often feel inundated with advertising materials No real power over upgrades or development process What happens if they go out of business?
Administration of site	Simple, easy to use Can choose number of administrators, e.g. one or everyone	Cannot personalize intranet, e.g. with logo or graphics
Calendar	Access to a calendar	
Polling facility	Enables participants to set up a poll or quiz Results are immediately collated and presented	
Document facility	Provides a shared document facility Simple, easy to use, takes a wide range of files Familiar folder structure Can add useful descriptive comments/messages Password facility enables differential access	Sometimes document size is limited and very small, e.g. 50K
Discussion facility	Provides an asynchronous discussion facility Simple, easy to use Able to view threading structure Password facility enables differential access	Sometimes lacks a new message or flag alert system
Instant messaging	Provides synchronous (real-time) discussion facility Simple, relatively easy to use Enables 1 to 1 and group conferencing	Sometimes tricky to use Sometimes lacks group conferencing facilities and only has 1 to 1 chat facilities Sometimes cannot make a copy of the transcript
Internet links	Simple, easy to use Provides easy access to each other's 'favourite' internet sites Can add useful descriptive comments/message	Sometimes no indexing/hierarchical features Sometimes difficult to structure and therefore if too many links are made it is time-consuming to search through a serial list

Continued

Table 3.2 *continued*

Facilities	Advantages	Disadvantages
Help facility	Simple online help system Clear and readable Access to additional support often available via e-mail	Limited or no help system

Virtual learning environments

Professional groups who wish to set up virtual learning communities in association with educational institutions such as universities or colleges are likely to find that they have access to a virtual learning environment (VLE) which is defined as follows:

> VLEs are web-based toolkits that facilitate learning through the provision and integration of online teaching and learning materials and tools. These materials and tools usually consist of most or all of the following: facilities for electronic communications such as discussion lists, bulletin boards and chat rooms, facilities for group work online; online learning materials; links to remote resources; course timetables and reading lists; online assessment tools; and an administrative area, including a log-in access function.
>
> INSPIRAL (2001)

Virtual learning environments (VLEs) provide all the facilities that are required to enable a virtual learning community to work together in a private meeting space. In many respects they replicate the facilities seen in physical organizations, as shown in Table 3.3.

Table 3.3 Comparison of virtual and physical organization of learning communities

Virtual environment	Physical equivalent
Discussion forum and conference rooms	Meeting rooms, discussions between colleagues
Notice or bulletin boards	Notice boards
Virtual cafés	Cafés, staff rooms, gatherings during tea breaks
Learning materials and resources	Library
Help desk	Help desk
Online quizzes, surveys	Use of questionnaires, votes
Monitoring and tracking systems	Diaries, signing in/out books and systems

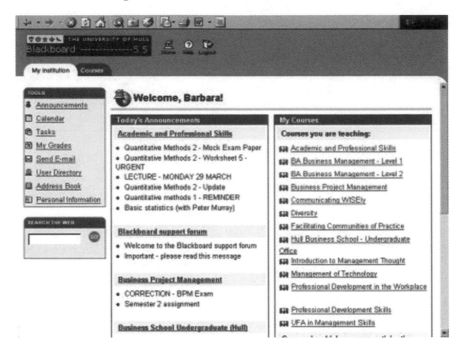

Figure 3.2   Home page of Blackboard

Common examples of virtual environments include: Blackboard (see Figure 3.2), WebCT, *Virtual Campus*. These learning environments are typically owned by the whole institution, who employ specialist staff to manage and administer these large and complex systems. Facilitators of virtual learning communities who have access to a VLE will find that they have access to a vast array of tools and these may be organized in such a way that the virtual learning community only has access to those tools that they need.

The range of tools that are available in a VLE are listed below and then described with reference to their use in a typical virtual learning community.

* Communication tools (see Figure 3.3).
* Information sources.
* Structured learning programmes.
* Assessment tools.
* Personal management tools.
* Administrator and tutor tools.

The communications facility normally provides access to the following tools:

* announcements or notice boards which are used to disseminate notices and files;
* a discussion board where facilitators and participants can communicate by leaving messages for each other (see Figure 3.4);

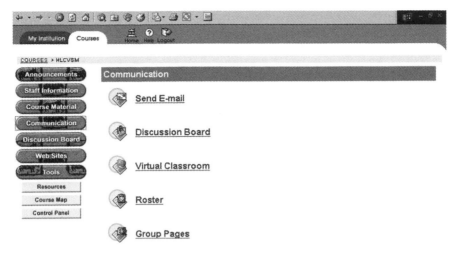

Figure 3.3   Blackboard communications tool page

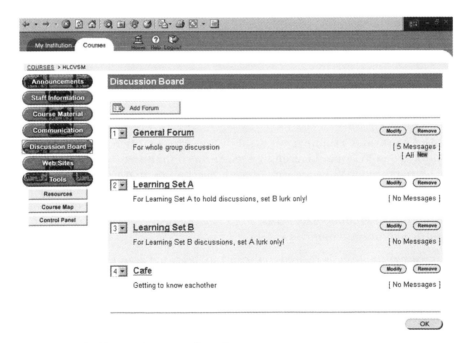

Figure 3.4   Blackboard discussion board

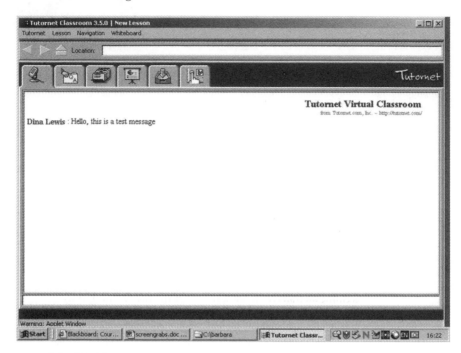

Figure 3.5   Blackboard chat room

- conference or chat rooms where individuals may hold a live chat session (see Figure 3.5);
- e-mail for individual or whole community e-mails.

Table 3.4 provides a summary of the different ways in which the communication tools in a VLE may be used by a learning community.

The majority of VLEs are designed in such a way that the learning community facilitator can provide access to information sources via direct or hot internet links (see Figure 3.6). Clicking on these links results in community members having immediate access to the resources via the screen. Examples of information sources include:

- information directly related to the virtual learning community;
- information about the organization or department;
- subject portals;
- national newspapers and information sources;
- search engines.

Although some VLEs enable individual community members to directly upload weblinks, in others they need to be entered by an administrator or facilitator who has the necessary set of permissions. In some instances this may cause a short delay in the whole community gaining access to the link.

Table 3.4 Use of VLE communication tools by a virtual learning community

Tool	Brief description	Application in virtual learning community
E-mail	Many VLEs provide e-mail facilities These may be limited to e-mailing members of a particular group and sending messages within the VLE, i.e. not external to it Also many VLEs provide an e-mail distribution list and users can send group e-mails without setting up their own distribution lists	Facilitator sends a private message to a group member Members send private messages to each other Members send group e-mails to remind community members of deadlines or new information available within the VLE
Notice or announcement boards	As their name suggests these enable facilitators to post notices to their learners. Some systems enable you to attach files to the notices	Facilitators use notice boards to inform members of news, meetings, new resources Effective for updating communities with important information
Discussion board	These provide a facility for discussion (much like an internet newsgroup) under various topic headings and not in real time. They allow virtual learning community members to respond to topics or threads in the group, or to begin a new topic or thread by posting a comment or question. Any messages sent to a discussion group are permanently visible to everyone who has access to it	These are used by virtual learning community members and facilitators to exchange information and ideas, to discuss and work on current issues or problems, and to construct knowledge
Conference or chat rooms	Conference rooms provide a 'real-time' conferencing facility (much like internet chat or a face-to-face seminar). Many conference rooms are text-based, although others provide facilities for sound and images too. They offer opportunities for 1 to 1 and also small group discussions	Conference or chat rooms are commonly used for 'live' meetings to discuss an urgent issue, a visiting expert may lead a discussion Live chats are often used for social purposes as participants often find the live aspect fun They are often used to revive a flagging group

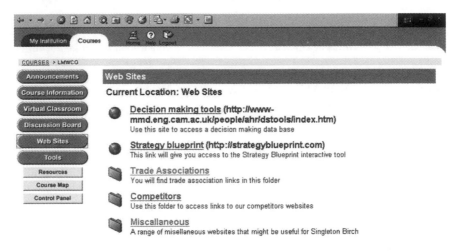

Figure 3.6   Example of a set of hyperlinks made available to a virtual learning community

Structured learning programmes include resources such as self-study materials, multimedia packages and also online assessment tools, questionnaires and inventories. The suppliers of VLEs often provide a standard bank of learning and training materials and the majority provide an online tutorial on using the VLE. Many virtual learning communities will not have any need for structured learning programmes but other virtual learning communities may find them relevant to their work.

VLEs offer a range of assessment tools such as online tests or quizzes and these are not always required by virtual learning communities. Some virtual learning communities find that they will use these tools as a means of carrying out research or obtaining information from each other. VLEs also provide a range of personal management facilities and these enable individual members to keep a diary, update their user details (such as a change in private e-mail address) and also change their password.

Virtual learning community facilitators require access to a control or tools facility (see Figure 3.7) and these are normally only available to specific users such as tutors, instructors and system administrators. They enable individuals to:

- create and manage groups;
- update and manage the virtual learning environment;
- monitor membership activity, for example login, length of time online, results of online assignments.

VLEs typically allow different types and levels of access: member, student or guest access; facilitator or tutor access; administrator or manager access. Each of these types of access enable the user to work in and manipulate the virtual environment. For example, virtual learning community members are

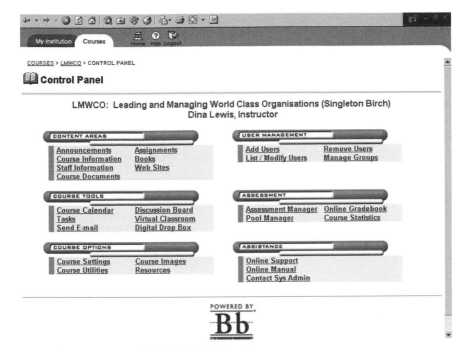

Figure 3.7   The control facility in Blackboard

typically allowed access to communication tools, information resources and personal management tools. Facilitators normally have access to the tools facility, including information about member enrolment and online activities, participant tracking information, for example details of logins and online work, assessment results. In contrast, administrator or manager access enables individuals to add new communities or programmes and provide access to the system to members and facilitators.

Summary

This chapter has outlined a range of different virtual communication tools and platforms. Virtual learning communities may rely on very simple tools such as e-mail or they may work within more sophisticated environments such as group communications software or virtual learning environments that provide a mixture of asynchronous and synchronous tools. It is important to remember that software tools and virtual learning environments are only a means to an end. Our experience of working with virtual learning communities has demonstrated that **facilitator input** rather than the technical capability of the system is the key to success. Just providing a range of online facilities and resources and creating an open forum for discussion will not automatically lead to the formation of learning communities; our assessment of whether a software system is effective is based on **how it is being used**. Without support and guidance on the pedagogy of online learning communities we firmly believe that the technology is of limited use.

4

The Community Life Cycle: Foundation and Induction Phases

Introduction

This chapter introduces the concept of the community life cycle, that is the distinctive phases of development that virtual communities experience from their inception to their closure or transformation into a new and different community. The virtual learning community life cycle is made up of six phases and the first two, foundation and induction, are explored in this chapter. The other phases are looked at in Chapters 5 and 6. In this chapter we will consider key questions for facilitators related to the foundation and induction stages of development and identify potential issues affecting these stages of development for both participants and facilitators.

The virtual learning community life cycle

All communities are dynamic, living and growing entities with shifting and changing aims and purposes. We have found it useful both as facilitators and community members to think of communities as having a life cycle with distinct developmental phases. This has helped us to understand the process of community development, to plan to support communities through identified phases of the life cycle and also to clarify potential issues and strategies for resolving them.

The following model was developed from our analysis of participant discussion contributions and qualitative data drawn from open focus groups and community evaluations. In the virtual community life cycle model (Figure 4.1) we have identified six distinct phases:

1   Foundation, p. 54
2   Induction, p. 63
3   Incubation, p. 73
4   Improving performance, p. 89

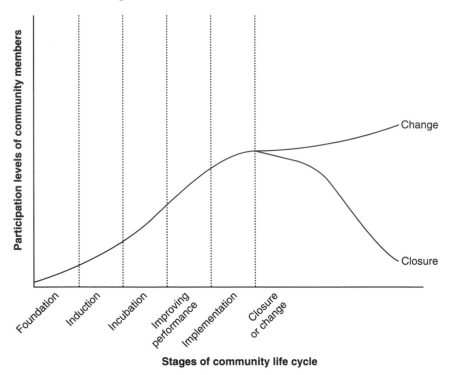

Figure 4.1   The virtual community life cycle model

The remainder of this chapter will focus on the first two stages: foundation and induction.

Phase 1 Foundation

Communities are formed in a variety of ways and for many different reasons. The stimulus that starts off a community may be:

- an individual with a specific purpose or goal in mind;
- a group of practitioners with a professional need to share good practice and exchange ideas; or often
- a sponsor or organization with a strategic plan to establish learning communities to support the implementation of change.

As previously discussed, some learning communities evolve organically, for example from a group of colleagues working together on a new project, and some may be created as part of a professional or strategic workforce development activity. Sometimes communities of interest such as an e-mail discussion list evolve into a learning community through the energy and commitment of a core group of enthusiasts. In some cases communities form slowly and over a period of time as a group of individuals come together and realize the value of working, learning and collaborating together.

Sometimes communities are sponsored, for example by an employer, professional association or other agency and in these cases it is likely that there will be a 'formal' foundation phase. This is likely to involve the sponsor(s), initiator(s) or facilitator(s) spending time planning and working out how the community will come together and interact. The facilitators and/or sponsors are likely to spend time developing and creating an information infrastructure that will support the community's information and knowledge requirements. At this stage there are distinct considerations:

- What is the purpose of the community?
- What is the structure of the community?
- Who are the potential community members?
- How will members work and learn together?
- What ICT infrastructure is required?
- What administrative support is required?
- What type of design is required for the virtual learning environment?

What is the purpose of the community?

Answering this question involves moving from a general understanding that it is a good idea to develop a learning community to spending some time identifying a specific aim or purpose. Communities are formed usually for the following reasons:

- To support the strategic implementation of workforce development.
- To enable practitioners to work and learn together on specific projects or issues.
- To bring practitioners together to develop further understanding of a particular field of knowledge – to provide a mechanism for the management and creation of new knowledge.
- To provide opportunities for practitioners to share good practice and develop skills and technical know-how.
- To provide an arena for networking and socializing with other practitioners with a shared interest and focus.

Some examples of communities that we have been involved in supporting during the 'foundation' phase are described in the three case studies in Box 4.1.

What is the structure of the community?

There are a number of different approaches to structuring and managing a virtual learning community and it is often helpful for the community facilitator and sponsor(s) to spend a little time working out the best type of

---

Box 4.1   Three case studies

Case study A: Work-based learning trainers' and tutors' learning community

This was formed to meet the professional development needs of a group of trainers/tutors working with dispersed work-based learning (WBL) students. The purpose of the community was to equip the trainers/tutors with the specific skills, knowledge and understanding to enable them to support WBL students dispersed over a large geographical area more effectively. The purpose of the community was also to establish a vibrant peer support group for the trainers. The facilitator identified that WBL students would benefit from being supported through a virtual learning environment and none of the WBL trainers or tutors had had experience in using a VLE to support dispersed work-based learners. The facilitator offered to run a short six-week programme inviting trainers to participate in a virtual learning community focusing on key issues in relation to e-learning pedagogy in order to equip tutors to use learning technologies to support learners in the workplace effectively. In this case the facilitator identified the need then offered to provide a virtual learning community training experience.

Case study B: Virtual learning communities within the NHS as a strategic response to service improvements in mental health

The purpose of the project was to provide an infrastructure to support dynamic learning communities and the model was designed as a strategic response to implementing mental health service improvements within the NHS in the Northern Region. In this case employers wanted strategic, innovative and more effective approaches to support the introduction of new work practices. We were involved in the design and implementation of the pilot project. This included training facilitators to support learning communities of senior managers within the NHS to engage in problem-based learning focusing on the implementation of the new service framework (NSF) within the mental health sector. The facilitators were trained to support learning communities using learning technologies with an emphasis on critical reflective practice.

Case study C: The escape committee

This community formed spontaneously by a group of professionals in crisis with similar career development needs. The purpose of the community was to enable members to obtain alternative employment, provide mutual support and sharing of good practice, and to provide a 'safe' space for discussions.

This 'escape committee' was formed by a group of individuals who all knew each other and worked within a public sector organization that was currently dramatically changing its culture and also downsizing. The community was established spontaneously after a discussion over a lunch break and members used it to share their *curriculum vitae* (and obtain feedback on them), exchange information and advice on applying for jobs and attending interviews, and generally give each other support. The learning community met through a virtual site using group software. An important aspect of the community was that it was an informal, voluntary, closed group and that it was password-controlled and so only accessible to group members. This community existed until the sixth (and last) member obtained a new position.

structure for the community. In Chapter 2 we explored three distinct community structures, that is simple, managed and complex, and these provide blueprints for the development of distinct types of communities. Alternatively individual facilitators or community sponsors may develop their own unique community structure.

Who are the potential community members?
In our experience virtual learning communities are likely to be effective if their membership is relatively small, that is 5 to 18 members, and if numbers grow beyond this then the likely result will be a community of interest is formed rather than a learning community. Sometimes the facilitator will identify appropriate members and invite them to join a community, at other times the members will have come together in response to a call for volunteers or in response to a change initiative or improvement plan. Employing organizations often take the initiative in supporting the development of communities bringing work colleagues from related areas together to work on particular problems or projects. In the NHS case study above a call for volunteers went out in a mental health services newsletter. Over 60 professionals from all service areas of mental health responded, including doctors, nurses, local government and social services managers and NHS commissioners, all of whom were keen to take part in the innovative approach to service improvements. This large group of professionals was broken down into six learning communities.

Box 4.2   Identifying potential members

Here is a list of questions to ask when identifying potential members.

- Who is likely to be interested in membership of this community?
- Who is likely to benefit from this community?
- Who is likely to be enthusiastic and contribute to the life of this community?

- Who has the appropriate range of knowledge, skills and experience?
- How will the community be resourced?
- Will participants be given 'work time' to participate. If not why not? If so, how will this be managed?
- Is the community proposed for a certain time span?
- Is the community expected to be active indefinitely?
- Who will facilitate the community?
- How will potential participants be identified/recruited? (Via general advertisement, for example workplace notice boards, virtual notice boards, personal recommendations, in a discussion group, personal invitation?)

How will members work and learn together?
At this initial stage it is worthwhile spending a little time thinking about how the community will operate. This could involve a blended mixture of face-to-face meetings and online communications, alternatively it may be an entirely online community. It is important to think through the implications of your decisions at this stage, for example face-to-face meetings may limit attendance of some community members due to work and other commitments. In contrast a virtual community is limited to people who have access to appropriate ICT equipment and also the time and the motivation to access the community regularly. Some participants may be uncomfortable or unfamiliar with technology.

In the NHS mental health case study above, each learning community met together six times a year face-to-face, the whole large community including all participants from each of the six learning communities also met six times a year to listen to guest speaker inputs from the Sainsbury Centre for Mental Health. The face-to-face meetings provided opportunities for the participants from across the different learning sets/communities to meet to share issues, problem-solving strategies and good practice.

Box 4.3   Community communications

Here are some questions for facilitators to ask when thinking about community communications.

- Will the community hold face-to-face meetings?
- If it will involve meetings then where, when and how often will they be arranged?
- Will the community use learning technologies?
- Will the community platform be open or closed to other participants?
- Will different groups and sub-groups have different access to particular areas?

- Will the community use a mixture of face-to-face and online communication?
- Do potential members have access to computers and the web?
- Do potential members have the technical confidence to use the ICT facilities?
- What are the likely technical requirements for the community? Will members be expected to have access to low-specification or high-specification hardware?
- Will there be support available for those experiencing technical problems?

What ICT infrastructure will support the community?

Information and communication technologies that are commonly used to support learning communities are outlined in Chapter 3. It is clear that ICT infrastructures now offer learning communities a wide range of new possibilities in supporting more flexible channels of communication, greater opportunities for information sharing and exciting collaborative approaches to knowledge management. Communities do exist successfully without an ICT infrastructure, but those communities that are designed around the use of online technologies have much greater flexibility.

When you consider your ICT needs then it is worthwhile answering the following two questions:

1 What type of ICT facilities will the learning community members have access to?
2 How could we use ICT to support our learning community most effectively?

The answer to the first question is important as the type of ICT facilities available to individual learning community members will impact on the way in which they can participate in that community. At a minimal level individual members will need easy access to the internet and they will need to be able to access remote sites several times a week. If your members are likely to have access to basic ICT equipment with slow internet access, then you are likely to be most successful if you restrict the learning community to using basic e-mail and communications software or systems. It can be very frustrating for individuals if they log into a system and find that pages or items take a very long time to download or if they constantly crash their system. In contrast if your learning community members have access to state-of-the-art ICT equipment and broadband internet access, then you will be able to consider using advanced communication tools involving whiteboards, video clips and video links.

The second question relates to thinking about how your community would use ICT to communicate with each other. Answering this question involves thinking about the types of activities that individual members may get involved in and common examples include:

- chat synchronously;
- post asynchronous discussions;
- attach and exchange files;
- share audio sound;
- look at website synchronously;
- group email.

Chapter 3 gives examples of the different types of facilities available in different ICT systems in more detail.

Technical support

You will also need to consider the issue of technical support and who provides it. If you are establishing a learning community within an organization that has an ICT department then it is likely that they will be able to provide technical help and support. If you are hosting and supporting the learning community yourself, for example as part of a project, then you will need to be very clear about the levels of technical support that are available. The authors' experience is that individuals who are new to using virtual communication tools need a certain level of technical support and that this can be extremely time consuming.

Over the years we have been involved in a wide range of communities where the lack of technical support has threatened the success of the whole community, the mental health project highlighted above was a good example. At that time the NHS ICT infrastructure in the Northern region was very patchy and participants in the learning communities had varying levels of technical support. In addition there were problems in working across the different organizations due to firewalls and internet connections. Not surprisingly, this had a direct impact on the success of the online communications within the communities. However, ICT infrastructures and systems are constantly improving and technical support within most organizations, including the NHS, is also improving. Recently, most of the technical queries our communities have encountered have been resolved without too much difficulty and we have found increasingly that participants within communities are advising each other on technical hitches. As facilitators we do not take responsibility for giving technical support, however we do assist participants in accessing the support that is available.

Box 4.4   Questions for facilitators when considering an ICT infrastructure

---

- What ICT facilities are available to members?
- What is the simplest ICT infrastructure we can use?
- How will the ICT infrastructure support the information and knowledge needs of the community?

- What will we want to be able to do online – e-mails, bulletin board, chat or conference rooms, exchange documents, use a whiteboard, polling?
- Will we have to buy new software or hardware? What will it cost?
- Will all of our potential members have access to this ICT?
- Will any participants need additional support and training in using ICT?
- Who will support the ICT?
- What technical support is available?
- If you are working across a number of different organizations then are their ICT systems compatible?

Administrative support

We have found it helpful to ensure that administrative support is available when we have worked with managed or complex learning communities. The role of the administrator involves supporting the community in a variety of ways, for example organizing face-to-face meetings, managing a virtual library of documents, chasing up reports and documents from members. An effective administrator can act as the lynch pin of the community.

Designing the virtual learning environment

At some stage before the start of the learning community the facilitator(s) and technical support staff will need to design the virtual environment. If the virtual community is developing its own website then the design of the environment is likely to involve extensive work. However, it is a relatively simple task if the community is going to use group communication software or a VLE and it will involve identifying the facilities required in the virtual learning community, for example announcements, discussion group, conference rooms, document store, polling facility. Many VLEs allow instructors/ facilitators to personalize the learning space using different colour combinations and through the addition of logos. In addition, the facilitator will need to ensure that all the information required for the induction process is available online (see next section). The designers of the virtual learning environment need to ensure that it is easy to navigate, usable and accessible. Once the site is designed then it will need to be evaluated for usability using a tool such as that found at http://www.uce.ie/hfrg/ questionnaires.

When working in a virtual environment community members need to know where they are, how they got there and where they can move to next. It is important that the materials are organized in a logical way and that guiding is available. The following facilities are often used to organize virtual learning communities:

- Home page with site map

- Search tools
- Help facility
- Menu of community facilities, for example discussion groups, conference rooms, information sources, hyperlinks.

An example home page is given in Figure 3.2 (page 46).

One decision that the learning community facilitators will need to make is whether or not to provide a virtual social area such as a café. These are often introduced early in the life of a community as they provide an area where community members can socialize, gossip and exchange jokes! Some facilitators like to integrate these activities into the main discussion threads while others believe that separating social chat into a separate discussion area encourages community members to initiate social interactions. Sometimes social areas are created as facilitator-free zones and provide a space for participants to chat freely without the involvement of the facilitator. We usually negotiate this with our learning communities during the induction stage of the community life cycle, offering members the choice of having an unmoderated area. One advantage of creating separate social areas is that individuals who are hard pressed for time can give the social area a miss.

It is really important that the virtual learning environment is readable and easy to use. There is nothing worse than being faced with indigestible chunks of dense reading material in a very small font. Factors that need to be considered include:

- Text is legible against the background
- Use of appropriate font style and size
- Text is surrounded by sufficient space – 'white space'
- Text is chunked into appropriate sizes, for example 5–6 points per chunk
- Long pages include a table of contents and a 'back to top' button
- Lists and bullet points are used rather than large blocks of text
- Minimal horizontal scrolling
- Maximize accessibility, for example provide large font versions, provide text of audio tapes.

It is also important that the text is accessible to a diverse group of community members, for example people with visual impairment. Further information on this specialist topic is available from The Web Accessibility Initiative at: http://www.w3.org/TR/WAI-WEBCONTENT/.

Getting started

The start of a learning community is likely to involve an organization or an individual taking the initiative and making sure that all potential members are contacted and advised of the new community. This process also needs to happen even if it is an existing learning community that is starting to use virtual communications in addition to more traditional meetings. Whatever the ICT infrastructure, the sponsoring organizations or the administrator or the facilitator will be involved in producing and circulating welcome letters and introductory documentation. It is important that individual members have all the relevant technical information, for example URL, user IDs and passwords as well as information about technical support. The administrator (in some cases this is also the facilitator) may be involved in telephoning likely members and discussing potential membership. Once people have signalled their intention to join the learning community then it is a good idea to obtain a mini-biography and also a photograph – these can be posted up in a virtual community rogues' gallery or group homepage. This forms a useful reference point, particularly during the induction stage when new group members are starting to get to know each other.

Phase 2 Induction

Once the sponsoring organization, or administrator or facilitator, has established the community and identified and agreed key parameters, for example identified community participants, communication methods, technical infrastructure, then the next phase of the life cycle is induction. This is the stage when the facilitator takes over control, facilitating the initial induction and interactions of the members. During the induction phase facilitators and participants are actively involved in exchanging factual information; this may be related to the proposed community, technical issues and also information of a more personal nature.

The facilitator will be extremely active throughout this phase reassuring participants and creating a safe and comfortable community environment. Much of the facilitator's work will be online, although they may also be involved in face-to-face sessions and telephone conversations with members. The induction phase could be started off online, however, wherever possible we always aim to start our virtual learning communities by a face-to-face induction session. This induction session includes workshop activities and a technical introduction to the software or virtual learning environment.

We find the following activities helpful during the induction phase:

- Introductions
- Narratives
- Technical introduction to the ICT infrastructure
- Ice-breakers
- Ground rules
- Surfacing and discussing hopes and fears of community members.

These activities can be facilitated online or face-to-face depending on the circumstances of the community and facilitator.

Personal introductions
Any induction phase should begin with introductions. Participants will need to introduce themselves to the other community members and we have found that it is really helpful if participants share information about their role at work and any special interests they may have. During face-to-face

sessions we encourage participants to introduce themselves online during the technical introduction to the ICT infrastructure, this activity is an important initial step in finding and creating an online voice and presence.

Most participants feel very wary at this early stage, they are concerned not to expose themselves too much. Facilitators need to be sensitive to the participants' feelings, it often helps if facilitators provide example information about themselves, just a few sentences to start the ball rolling and setting an informal tone. Participants' introductions are really valuable as they provide a useful reminder and reference during the early stages when facilitators and participants are trying to remember individuals and construct an identity for fellow participants. This is particularly important if the community is larger than six participants as it can be very difficult to construct an identity for each member, particularly if there hasn't been a face-to-face induction session. Photographs also help participants and facilitators to get to know each other but we have found that many participants are reluctant to make their photograph available online.

Examples of facilitator's and participant's introductions are given in Boxes 4.5 and 4.6.

Box 4.5   Example of facilitator's introduction

Hello everyone,

I am really looking forward to this opportunity to work with you as a co-facilitator of the managers' learning community. I've worked with Barbara Allan on a number of projects in the public and private sector but this will be the first time that we have worked with colleagues in the steel industry. I hope there will be an opportunity for a site visit.

I work at the University of Hull as the Programme Director for Work-Based Learning programmes and my research interest is focused on the potential of e-learning to improve practice in the workplace.

In my spare time I enjoy the rigours of family life (we've four kids approaching independence), travel (without offspring) and walking in the Yorkshire Dales.

In addition to the VLE online community I can be contacted on:

D. Lewis@hull.ac.uk or phone 0123 456789

I look forward to working with you.

All the best,
Dina

Box 4.6   Example of participant's introduction

Hello folks!

I'm Project Support Officer for the University of Ambridge Learning Development Unit. My previous background has been mainly administrative. I've supported various members of the Senior Management Team in Information Services and worked as a Project Administrator for the ****** project.

I have been at Ambridge for just over three years and really enjoy my work. I currently support Project Leaders, a number of whom are participating in this community. My role is very varied and the level of support given to Project Leaders is very dependent on their needs. Some projects remain fully self-managed while others require a lot more support.

About me. I enjoy socializing, don't do any sport although I should, and LOVE food, any time/type/amount (I also love McDonald's!) I have two cats, one of which weighs 7.1 kilos and lost his first tooth recently, the other is neurotic and a pain in the butt! I am really enjoying being involved in this learning community and find it great to be learning again. (It's been a while!) I'm still finding my way around WebCT as both a learner and an administrator. Some of you seem to be able to make very flash homepages. I'm still trying. I'm having technical difficulties importing PDFs into FrontPage. I'll get there . . . one day.

Cheers
Sam

Narratives

Narratives can also play a valuable role in encouraging participants to get to know each other and find an 'online voice'. We often invite participants to work in pairs and share a significant experience from their own lives, for example, a work-related problem, a positive learning experience or an example of a successful collaborative learning experience. Wenger (1998) emphasizes the importance of narrative to the social integration of communities of practice, he gives many examples of workers sharing work experiences through the narrative form and his research indicates that there is a link between the use of narratives and the social cohesion of the community. We have found, without a doubt, that narratives can promote social cohesion and encourage the sharing of perceptions and precepts in a non-threatening way.

Technical induction

We have also found during the induction phase that it is important to provide a technical induction to the ICT facilities. It is important to note that
participants often forget technical instructions and information, particularly
information and instruction given during the first face-to-face induction
meeting.

During face-to-face induction sessions we usually invite a technician or an
IT trainer to deliver a short practical session in an IT lab. Our experience
has shown that participants definitely benefit from a hands-on exploration of
the functions and facilities of the ICT infrastructure. Sometimes one session
is not enough and we arrange for the participants to have a follow-up session
within a week or two so that any technical difficulties that arise can be
resolved quickly and effectively. However, this is not always possible and for
those groups that are inducted online we make use of online wizards and
online interactive guides to software facilities. Step-by-step instructions
available in hard copy are also very useful.

Ice-breakers

Most facilitators and participants have mixed feelings about the value of
online 'ice-breakers' or social games to encourage the group to get to know
each other. We both use ice-breakers regularly with face-to-face groups, yet
have both felt reluctant to use ice-breakers and games online. During our
early encounters with online learning communities we were swept along by
the sheer enthusiasm of our participants to engage in the serious business of
online working and learning. However, evaluations of those groups revealed
that some of the participants missed out on the essential social interactions
that lead to trust and openness within a community. Facilitators need to give
careful thought to designing activities that will encourage participants to gel
socially at this stage. One example of an activity that we have used successfully with a number of virtual learning communities is the 'Desert activity',
see Box 4.7.

Box 4.7   Desert activity

Your group is attempting to cross the Sahara Desert and your mini-bus
has broken down. A magician appears with the following list of items.
He is prepared to donate five of these items to the whole team.

torch (4 battery size)
bottle of salt tablets (1000)
jack-knife
1 quart of water per person
sectional air map of crash area
book entitled *Edible Animals of the Desert*
plastic raincoat

2 pairs of sunglasses per person
magnetic compass
2 quarts of 180° proof vodka
bandage kit with gauze
1 overcoat per person
45 calibre pistol
cosmetic mirror
parachute (red and white)

What you need to do

Individually, you need to identify your top five items and your reasons for selecting them. You need to share your thinking with the group.

Then working as a team you have to select your team's top five items. The magician says that the selection should be based on consensus, that is a group decision-making process. Consensus is difficult to reach. Therefore, not every ranking will meet with everyone's complete approval. Try, as a team, to make each ranking one with which all team members can at least partially agree. Here are some guides to use in reaching consensus:

1. Avoid arguing for your own individual judgements. Approach the task on the basis of logic.
2. Avoid changing your mind only in order to reach agreement and avoid conflict. Support only solutions with which you are able to agree somewhat, at least.
3. Avoid 'conflict-reducing' techniques such as majority vote, averaging or trading in reaching decisions.
4. View difference of opinion as helpful rather than as a hindrance in decision making.
5. View your initial agreement as suspect.

Once you have decided on your top five team items then post a team message with the thread name 'The magician' by noon on Thursday.

This ice-breaking activity could easily be adapted to involve the participants in a work-related prioritizing exercise, for example contents of a paramedics medical kit when dealing with a specific accident or tool kit for engineers dealing with a specific type of machine breakdown, etc.

Original source unknown.

If you are considering using an ice-breaker with your community then it is worthwhile using the list of questions shown in Box 4.8 to help ensure that it is an effective activity.

Box 4.8   Questions for facilitators when using ice-breakers

Is this activity appropriate for my group?
Is it work-related?
Will this activity encourage informal interactions and collaborative learning?
Will my group enjoy this activity?
Are the instructions clear and easy to follow?
Will the group feel comfortable doing this activity?
How can I encourage them to extend their comfort zones?

Ground rules
Our experience with virtual learning communities has highlighted the need to establish ground rules during the induction phase. Establishing ground rules is a useful way of enabling individual members to start to take ownership of the community as they can explicitly define and agree expectations in terms of community behaviour. Ground rules also enable variations in expectations between individual members to be raised and explored, for example one member may anticipate accessing an online community once or twice a month while another member may expect interactions on a daily basis. Identifying and resolving these differences is an important precursor to successful community development. If the behaviour of individual members later becomes a problem, participants can be reminded of the original ground rules agreed by each member and this can help to restore standards of behaviour, for example in the use of inappropriate language or the need for all views to be accepted and considered. We have always encouraged groups to spend some time considering their own ground rules: each community will have specific and different requirements. However, there are generic topics that are relevant to most communities and the facilitator can offer helpful prompts on the following topics:

- Confidentiality
- Frequency of online participation
- Respect for others
- Avoidance of abusive language.

The following examples, Box 4.9, illustrate the type of posting a facilitator may use to initiate a discussion and also examples of typical sets of ground rules.

The following two sets of ground rules, Box 4.10, were developed in two learning communities facilitated by the authors.

Box 4.9   Example of a facilitator's posting encouraging the community to agree ground rules

---

Hello everyone

At the beginning of a new virtual learning community it is helpful to agree a set of ground rules for group participation. At this stage it is usually helpful for members to make explicit and agree their expectations for online participation. Examples of ground rules that you might find helpful are:

(a) For the group to agree a minimum frequency of participation, with a learning set such as this it is important that the group agrees to participate regularly.
(b) Confidentiality – anything discussed within this area is confidential to the group.

Please make your own suggestions for ground rules for participation in this learning community and also comment on each others' suggestions.

Thanks very much
Dina

Box 4.10   Examples of community ground rules

Ground rules for steel works managers

Respect for individuals
Access site a minimum of three times a week
Spelling mistakes are acceptable
Respect for varying speeds of typing
Use meaningful titles for threads
No abusive language
Nominate a facilitator for chat-room sessions
Confidentiality within the group would be good
Respect the right of other members to hold alternative opinions

Ground rules for health professionals

We all agree to check out the blackboard at least twice a week and most of us will aim for three times a week (any less than this and you will be in danger of missing out on activities)
Confidentiality is an agreed underpinning principle
We will encourage succinct written contributions
We will aim to be focused and avoid procrastination

Speling is not an issue and we will not make judgements about typoss and speling errers

We recognize and respect the differing levels of experience and technical competence within the group

We will avoid gossip and encourage and support less confident and verbal members of the group

All opinions will be valued equally, we aim to nurture tolerance

Humour is to be encouraged, we want the experience to be enjoyable

Members will be encouraged to ask for and offer help

We want to encourage the whole community to grow and thrive: sub-communities should be discouraged

Everyone agrees to contribute to every activity whenever possible

You will note that there are distinct similarities between the two lists even though the communities had very different purposes and very different member profiles.

Community expectations

During the induction phase it can also be helpful to encourage participants to express their expectations of the community, this often involves participants in voicing their hopes and fears. It is surprising how many 'fears' participants voice if given the opportunity. Common fears or concerns include:

- fear of not being able to keep up with other members;
- fear of not having the same levels of expertise as other practitioners in the community;
- fear of technical skills letting them down;
- fear of being embarrassed by poor spelling or grammar.

The list of hopes and fears shown in Box 4.11 was generated by a virtual learning community whose members included health professionals, academics and training managers.

Box 4.11   Example list of hopes and fears

This list was developed at the beginning of a learning community designed to introduce NHS trainers and training managers to the potential of online learning communities as part of the WDC's implementation of their e-learning strategy.

Hopes

To ensure that e-learning is a positive experience
To be able to influence strategy for the NHS technical infrastructure in the region

That support systems for us as learners on the programme will be effective

To reach and engage non-traditional learners, in fact all potential users in our area

To coordinate development of e-learning nationally, though initially regionally including coordination of learning materials

Coordinate the provision of e-learning on a huge geographical scale

To sustain outcomes from this programme; to develop a strategy that is sustainable

To make accessible another training mode, for example 'blended approaches to learning'

That we will develop the ability, skills, knowledge and understanding to set up our own learning communities

Use e-learning to influence practice in the workplace and influence NHS strategy

To be able to integrate learning from this programme into other training practices within the NHS

Fears

Infrastructure – funding, concerns about support, additional workload

Time commitment, that we won't be given time release to undertake the programme

Sufficient time won't be allowed for us to implement the next phase of cascading the training

Access to computers for learners in the NHS

Not coping with the pressure of the programme – workload

e-learning coordinators fear participants will drop out

That the technology won't work

Feelings of isolation of participants on programme

ICT skills of staff that we will train in second phase

The facilitator will need to encourage openness in discussing any issues that arise. A discussion around different types and levels of participation may be useful at this stage. During the community closure phase it is useful to return to the original hopes and fears lists, and discussion around the induction hopes and fears of the community can make a valuable contribution to the community evaluation process.

Fears associated with technical difficulties need to be addressed during the early stages of community formation and we have discussed the need for technical support earlier in this chapter. We have also found it helpful to provide a discussion thread/forum within the community virtual discussion area specifically for technical queries during the induction phase (see Figure 3.1, p. 39). Facilitators will need to respond to technical queries very quickly in order to maintain ICT confidence within the group. Sometimes this response may be to refer participants to other sources of technical help. In our experience facilitators don't need to be able to answer every query but they do need to assure participants that they will refer participants to appropriate help or that they will follow up the query and get back to them as soon as possible.

The facilitator will be extremely active throughout the induction phase as their role is to ensure that individuals joining the learning community become comfortable within the virtual environment and confident about finding help and support if they do experience difficulties. Time spent resolving technical issues during the induction phase will benefit the effectiveness of the community later.

Summary

The life cycle of virtual learning communities is made up of the following stages: foundation; induction; incubation; improving performance; implementation; and closure or change. The facilitator is particularly active in the first two stages as they set up the necessary structures and systems to enable the community to come together and then facilitate the induction process. This results in a nascent virtual learning community that will then move into the incubation phase described in the next chapter.

5

The Community Life Cycle: Incubation Phase

Introduction

This chapter builds on the concept of the life cycle of a community and progresses some of the themes further by considering conditions for the growth and development of a new community during the incubation phase. It is important that facilitators recognize the unique needs of their community and then respond to them in an appropriate manner. In this chapter we identify and explore the four conditions of healthy and growing communities. We also investigate the contributions of members and facilitators in nurturing the four conditions of healthy and growing communities.

Phase 3 Incubation

During the incubation phase community members start to communicate, develop confidence in their online voice and they start to work together. The group begins to develop trust and often disclose and discuss their concerns. Community members often report that they lack confidence at this stage and feel reluctant to expose their perceived personal weaknesses to the whole group. The incubation phase is an important stepping stone in the life cycle of the community as unless members develop trust and share their real concerns then these may lie at the heart of many barriers to constructive development later on. The facilitator will need to take a proactive role supporting and encouraging members to engage actively in open discussions and guided activities. Paired activities that require members to share information and experience and begin to tackle work-related problems can work well. Facilitators need to incubate their communities during the early phase, taking care to respect comfort zones and not to challenge members too much too quickly. The incubation phase is about comfort and confidence, and encouraging the community to grow and develop through mutually supportive ways of working.

Identifying the unique needs of your community

During the incubation phase, effective facilitators recognize the unique needs of their communities and adopt nurturing strategies to meet these needs. Effective members also recognize the unique contribution that they can make to help their communities to grow towards their full potential as environments for dynamic learning and collaborative knowledge creation. In order to support the unique needs of their community facilitators might find the prompt questions in Box 5.1 useful.

Box 5.1   Questions for facilitators

1. Who are the confident communicators?
2. Who are the confident practitioners?
3. Are there professional hierarchies within the group?
4. Are there individual tensions?
5. Are the members collaborating; if not why not?
6. Are there technical difficulties/issues?
7. What roles are beginning to emerge within the community?
8. Will you allocate roles within the community? If so how?
9. Is humour evident?
10. Are suggestions for improvements welcomed?
11. Are you guiding from the side and emphasizing collective responsibility?
12. Do you intend to initiate learning activities?
13. If so, how can you ensure that the learning activities are relevant and engaging?
14. Are you monitoring individual access rates?
15. If members are not accessing the community, will you contact them?
16. Are you monitoring participation levels; some members may be accessing but not participating?
17. Are there any members who are not posting messages or responding to requests?
18. If so, do you intend to contact them privately to see if they need additional support?
19. How are you supporting those lacking in:
    (a) Social confidence?
    (b) Technical confidence?
    (c) Practitioner confidence?
20. Are the ground rules working?
21. As a facilitator what are your levels of activity? Are these appropriate within this community?
22. Are you enjoying your role within the community? If not, then what do you need to do?

The following questions in Box 5.2 can also be used to encourage members to reflect on their participation within the virtual learning community.

Box 5.2   Questions for members

1. Are you adhering to the ground rules?
2. Are you committed to the community?
3. Are your participation levels appropriate?
4. Do you feel comfortable? If not, why not?
5. Do you have any suggestions for improvements?
6. Is this experience fun?
7. What do you need to do to improve your work within the virtual learning community?
8. Who seems to be having difficulty?
9. Who are the low participators?
10. Can you offer support to anyone in particular?
11. Who do you have personal difficulty with?
12. What do you think of the facilitation skills of the facilitator? Would constructive feedback be appropriate?

Although the questions from Box 5.1 are designed to identify issues during the 'incubation' phase of the community life cycle, as learning communities evolve and mature their needs are also likely to change. We suggest that you will probably find it helpful to ask the prompt questions at regular intervals during the life cycle of your community as part of an ongoing review process.

The four conditions of healthy and growing communities

During the 'incubation' phase facilitators need to concentrate on supporting the community to grow and develop. Through our work with communities in the early stages of development, both as facilitators and members, we have identified four specific conditions that promote the healthy growth of communities and these are:

1   **Commitment and trust** Without commitment and trust most communities flounder. Successful communities have an atmosphere of trust and commitment and members feel that their open and honest contributions are valued and accepted.
2   **Comfort zones** Most members cite the importance of comfort zones. Successful communities offer members a comfort zone yet also enable members to take risks and follow learning trajectories that lead them beyond the security of their comfort zone.

3   **Collective responsibility and co-dependency**   These are key conditions
for healthy growth. Facilitators and members feel that the life of the
community is a shared responsibility, facilitators guide from the side and
members take the initiative when appropriate.
4   **Humour and fun**   These are such a bonus. Effective communities enjoy
themselves and there is shared humour; a sense of fun enhances shared
understanding and good working relationships.

These conditions are not exact fixed states, inevitably they vary according to
the different needs of different groups. There are, however, activities
and strategies that facilitators and members can employ to encourage
communities to promote these 'conditions'.

Condition 1   Commitment and trust
Commitment is a key condition of effective communities. Commitment is a
two-way process and the commitment of the facilitator is not enough to
ensure the success of a community. Committed facilitators can be key in
nurturing and modelling behaviours that lead communities towards
sustainable growth, as we can see from the example in Box 5.3.

Box 5.3   An NHS virtual learning community

We facilitated a short learning community training programme
designed to train six facilitators in online facilitation skills at the
same time as they facilitated learning communities of NHS professionals implementing service improvements. It was an innovative project with incredibly tight deadlines and this model of simultaneous
training and implementation was unprecedented. Formative and
summative evaluations highlighted a number of reasons why this model
of simultaneous training and implementation was flawed and why two
of the six facilitated learning communities were more successful
than the others. One of the key weaknesses identified was the pressure
this model placed on the facilitators; however, facilitator commitment
was the main distinguishing feature of the two online communities that
were most successful.

Of the facilitator group that we were training two were seriously
committed, giving time and energy to the online training and three
expressed interest but gave intermittent time and effort to the online
training and one avoided all contact with the online community both
within the training programme and also in communicating with his
learning community. The impact on facilitators' learning communities
was clear. The two committed facilitators ran online communities
which were prepared to overcome technical difficulties in the early
stages of online communication, their community members actively
participated in online synchronous conferences and openly shared
implementation strategies through online discussion postings. Not

---

surprisingly, the three facilitators with minimal commitment to the virtual training programme facilitated online groups that had serious problems with the levels of commitment to online communication and these groups expressed more frustration with the technology. The group with the facilitator who did not use the VLE made a few attempts to communicate online and gave up. The commitment of the facilitators had a marked impact on the commitment of the learning sets.

The example above demonstrates the importance of facilitator commitment. However, successful communities are interdependent on the commitment of both facilitators and members. Undoubtedly our most successful learning communities have been distinguished by the commitment of our participants.

Trust is also a key condition of effective communities and facilitators can take deliberate actions to nurture the development of trust within a virtual learning community. We considered ground rules during the 'induction' phase and explored the importance of encouraging members to subscribe to certain standards of behaviour. Ground rules focused on confidentiality and honesty are particularly helpful in supporting an atmosphere of trust within a community. When members feel that they can openly share thoughts and feelings, in an environment that offers non-judgmental acceptance, trust is likely to develop. Respect also leads to trust, and facilitators and members have a responsibility to ensure that respect is an underpinning expectation of all group interactions. Facilitators can demonstrate respect for members in a wide range of ways.

In the following posting (Box 5.4) the facilitator offers reassurance and validation for the member's negative feelings and she values the member's honest responses and emphasizes the importance of feelings within the learning process.

Box 5.4   Facilitator posting encouraging an atmosphere of respect and trust

Hello Janet

I thought I'd respond to your comment that to your group work felt like a mild disaster. Online groupwork is often messy and my experience is that it can often feel out of control. I'm slowly coming to the conclusion that there is something about online groupwork that is inherently more messy than face-to-face groupwork. To me this often feels uncomfortable as I like to work in a controlled way. Virtual groupwork whether it is on a course or part of a collaborative project is often given lower priority than face-to-face work. It would be interesting to see if there was any research data on this issue.

I was also interested in your comments: 'I'm glad we didn't distribute different parts of the task for each of us, since we engaged in a really valuable "conversation" about our readings. For me, this was more important and interesting than our product itself.' and I think this is one of the real values of collaborative groupwork. It's about discussing and coming up with a new understanding of the topic. The process is often more important than the final product.

My personal view is that the feelings side is very important. To me it is important that I enjoy working with others in an online group. It helps make the experience 'real'. I am a member of an online group and was in a bad car accident last year. I was really touched when one of the group members offered to visit me (200-mile round trip) to give me a hand with our project. Such a generous offer. It gave me a very nice feeling and has helped keep me motivated to work in that group. So in response to your question 'Does that count?' my very loud answer is 'yes'.

Best wishes
Barbara

Condition 2 Developing comfort zones
During the early stages of any community it is also important to create an atmosphere of safety and comfort. The need to feel comfortable is a recurrent theme in many online postings during the initial stages of induction. A few examples of postings on this theme are given in Box 5.5.

Box 5.5   Comfort zones

Posting 1 Jerry

'In response to the question about how I feel about this programme at the moment. I need to feel in a "comfort zone" it's ridiculous I know but I'm inhibited by the length of other members' contributions or quality of linguistic and grammatical style. I'm trying to feel confident to be myself, and contribute in my own unique way in the time that I have available but it's not easy. Encouraging words from the facilitator have really helped. My IT skills are improving, in fact I'm getting really sad . . . I was online at 10.30 on Saturday night last weekend.

Jerry

Posting 2 Barry

I am starting to feel comfortable taking part in discussion rooms and accessing the really useful information and contributing to threads. Its good to see others also have concerns, doubts, issues, etc. Thanks ****** for encouraging people to be honest and say what they think, as this has started the ball rolling and we're responding and empathizing with each other now. I'm finding this group really helpful already.

Barry

Posting 3 Polly

Hi Liz and Sue,

I do relate to your feelings during the first couple of weeks of this online community, especially being unsure of myself in relation to the group, this is unusual for me as I very rarely feel that way when in face-to-face situations. Like so many people who communicate effortlessly verbally, I am now stuck for something to write. I am very conscious that this is a course and I feel I need to prove myself and this seems to be inhibiting natural flow in discussion or that is how I feel. Accessing the technical system has been relatively easy but I get the feeling that other people are also slightly self-conscious. Feeling this way is impacting on my ability to take part and my confidence levels go up and down.

I really hope that this will become a real aid to learning and to finding useful information.

Polly

We have found that comfort zones are formed when members feel able to acknowledge their feelings, this includes positive and negative feelings. Opening and encouraging discussions about feelings and fears are often a good starting point. Members need to find an online voice and for some members this does not happen quickly. Some members will feel confident and able to make positive contributions in sharing expertise and supporting other members immediately and there will be those who feel uncomfortable, exposed and vulnerable, due in part to the expertise of their fellow members. The most effective way of ensuring that communities have an inclusive 'atmosphere' is to nurture an atmosphere of safety and comfort.

Once we have established a comfort zone where members feel able to speak openly and honestly with confidence and feelings of self worth, the challenge then is to encourage them to go beyond the protection of their comfort zone and engage in learning trajectories that will impact on their identity both as individuals and also as professionals. There is no linear progression, learners need to be able to move naturally in and out of their comfort zones; meeting with like-minded members can become like returning to a safe haven.

The example shown in Box 5.6 tracks an individual member's personal journey. The first posting is an example of a typical posting during the incubation phase, a discussion has been created where she can admit her fears and honest misgivings. The second posting demonstrates her confidence growing almost imperceptibly and the third posting shows her feelings about the comfort that the community offers once she has entered the improving performance phase.

Box 5.6   An individual journey

Posting 1

1 January 2002

Hello Everyone

   I agree with you Fred, I feel intimidated every time I log in. I started logging in every two or three days or so but now dread what I'll come into if I leave it more than a day. It's not just the discussions for me, I was late in on the last two tasks as I wasn't keeping up with what was happening. I also felt intimidated with the last activity where the level of thought and output was exceptionally high . . .

Posting 2

2 February 2002

She later reflects

. . . I suspect that in any learning community you will have a sub-group who take the learning further than is absolutely necessary and take the opportunity to push themselves and their knowledge further than is absolutely necessary. I suspect that we might have more of this type of people than is usual here in this community . . .

Posting 3

3 June 2002

Hi Everyone

Just thought that I should share my thoughts. I now think of this community as my bolt hole, being able to discuss things here is keeping me sane at the moment. As some of you know, I've been having a really tough time here at work recently, it's been like banging my head against a brick wall, some of my colleagues are unbelievably hostile. It's just so good to be able to talk to you guys and feel that I'm communicating with like-minded enthusiasts who share my professional values. So this is what a learning community feels like . . .

Thanks guys

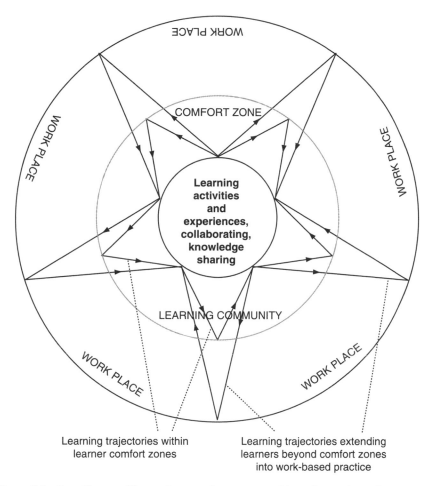

Learning trajectories within
learner comfort zones

Learning trajectories extending
learners beyond comfort zones
into work-based practice

Figure 5.1   Star diagram illustrating comfort zones and learning trajectories

We have found it helpful to visualize the concept of comfort zones as a
diagram (Figure 5.1). It seems that once a comfort zone has been established within a community, members use it as a launching pad, retreating
to the security and comfort of being with like-minded professionals when
the going gets tough. Members use their community comfort zone to gain
the strength and confidence to initiate: learning trajectories, work practices, innovations and solutions outside the community in the real world of
their work and professional lives, these activites take them way beyond the
secure boundaries of the community. This process of bursting out into
innovation and improved performance and then returning to the community is a recurrent pattern for many individuals in many different
communities.

Condition 3   Collective responsibility and co-dependency

Online learning is a relatively new process and one that is changing traditional tutor roles within higher education. Our experience demonstrates that this shift in roles is not exclusively limited to higher education and we have found that the interactions within virtual learning communities are changing the roles of trainers, facilitators, experts and project leaders in a wide range of public and private sector organizations in much the same way. Goodyear (2000) provides a useful framework to demonstrate how traditional higher education tutor roles are evolving and changing and we think this is just as relevant to virtual learning communities outside higher education. Attitudes towards tutors, trainers, leaders or 'experts' in the field are shifting and the function that they perform within learning communities is being redefined. Goodyear talks of a shift from 'sage on the stage' to 'guide on the side' (Table 5.1). During the incubation phase facilitators need to model behaviours that guide from the side and encourage members towards autonomy and collaborative working. Successful learning communities no longer accept the barriers to learning imposed by traditional hierarchical structures.

This concept of '*guide on the side*' is supported by research summarized by McCabe (1998) which suggests that in online groups there is a greater equality of participation with facilitators providing a much smaller input than in a face-to-face group. McCabe quotes figures of facilitator participation of 10 to 15% and 22%. In an online context facilitators may be involved in the following types of activities:

- Providing only the initial structure to groupwork;
- Encouraging increasing self-direction;
- Presenting multiple perspectives on topics;
- Highlighting and emphasizing the salient points.

Table 5.1 Shift from tutor to facilitator (from Goodyear 2000)

Traditional tutor/trainer roles		Online facilitator roles
'*sage on the stage*'	⟵——⟶	'*guide on the side*'
Lecturer	⟵——⟶	Consultant, guide, and resource provider
Providers of answers	⟵——⟶	Expert questioner
Providers of content	⟵——⟶	Designers of student learning experiences
Solitary tutor	⟵——⟶	Member of a learning team
Total control of the teaching environment	⟵——⟶	Shared control with the student as fellow learners
Total power over the teaching experience	⟵——⟶	Shared power with the students

Learning within the context of a community involves a process of shared interaction which involves community members and facilitator(s) discussing and developing their ideas in the process of knowledge construction. The facilitator is likely to learn as much from the process as the participants.

Effective facilitators use the range of expertise within the community to provide maximum support. They utilize the rich resources of expertise available within the community and do not take responsibility for all community needs. Effective 'incubation' is about encouraging members to help each other. This involves the facilitator in enabling and empowering community members to help and support each other. At times this means that the facilitator must hand a query or issue to the group to resolve rather than moving in with their own 'solution'. The following example illustrates one way in which this type of approach will work in practice.

In the Birmingham e-learning community members came from a range of different professional backgrounds (academics, technicians, librarians, administrators) and we encouraged members to have collective responsibility for the community. Individual members offered their own expertise as and when it seemed appropriate, for example technicians supported other group members with technical problems. During the early stages of community life we set up a discussion thread for technical queries. This was used frequently at first and we encouraged the technical members of the community to lead and support the less technically proficient members, we encouraged co-dependency as part of our 'incubation' strategy. Box 5.7 shows an example of one of the Birmingham University members offering technical help to other members.

Box 5.7   Example posting

Reply
Message no. 535 Posted by James B on Monday, January 14, 2002, 14:20

As promised, here is a more detailed explanation of the use of html in WebCT discussions. If you want to include a hyperlink in a discussion posting, you need to type the correct html syntax for a hyperlink when you are composing your message. For example, to include a link to the University's home page, you would type the following in the message composition box:

Link to the <a
href="http://www/bham.ac.uk"> University of
Birmingham</a>

and this is what will appear when the message is displayed:

Link to the University of Birmingham

> If you want to use hyperlinks, or bold text, etc. in discussions but don't feel confident about using html in your messages, here is a tip which might make things easier. Even if you know nothing about html, I imagine that most people here have used FrontPage to add hyperlinks to simple webpages. If you're not sure of the correct syntax for the html you want to use in your discussion posting, let FrontPage do it for you. Open FrontPage, start a new document and in Normal view write your text, then using the options from the FrontPage menu create the hyperlink or add the text formatting. When you're happy with the way it looks, change to the HTML view in FrontPage and you'll see the html version, which you can then cut and paste into the WebCT message screen.

This process of mutual support and co-dependence was modelled in other aspects of the community's activities, we utilized the professional expertise of the participants and encouraged individuals to lead activities when appropriate. The community was strengthened by this model of interaction.

Condition 4 Humour
Humour can be vital to the health and well-being of a community. Given the lack of non-verbal signals within virtual communities the use of humour can be very finely balanced and we would recommend that facilitators use humour with care during the early stages of community development. However, humour really can incubate community bonding. In an ideal world we have found that it is quicker and easier to encourage humour during face-to-face sessions and then capitalize on this afterwards online.

An active and loquacious member of one of our communities missed the initial induction session and therefore we had not met him face-to-face. During the early stages of his community's development we both noted that some of his postings seemed peremptory and pompous, and as facilitators we weren't sure how to take some of his comments. We decided to monitor his contributions carefully and reserve our judgements. This was just as well as when we met the community face-to-face for the second time it became clear that this member was, in fact, very jovial with a keen sense of irony and humour. The virtual vacuum in which online communities communicate had not allowed his natural sense of fun to come over. After the meeting we commented on the fact that he was so much more jovial in the flesh and from that point onwards he was instrumental in initiating many instances of humour within the group. His ebullient contributions really did 'gel' the group and nurture goodwill amongst the members (see Box 5.8).

Box 5.8   Example use of humour

Dear All,

Just to prove it can be done and as promised, here is the news from sunny Dhaka! In response to Barbara and Dina's question about having a good weekend, no I didn't.

I left my house at 10am on Friday. Everything went swimmingly. I was on the plane, settled on my seat when some duffer jammed a luggage container in the hold. Delayed for three hours. Three hours later, we left the plane. Delayed again. More delays. Hotel Metropole. Plane leaves in the morning. 2am wake up call. 7am flight.

Left Birmingham eventually at 7.45. Arrived Dubai 6pm. 'Sorry, Sir, the next flight to Dhaka is at 02.50, didn't they tell you this in Birmingham?' No they bloody didn't.

Finally arrived in Dhaka 24 hours late on Sunday morning. Sunday is a working day in Dhaka. I had to attend several meetings with serious people pretending that I was both awake and knew what they were talking about.

Do you know what I had to read on the plane? Do you? Gilly Salmon's book. I am sick of E-tutoring. Only joking.

Hopefully will be able to post something more meaningful later in the week to my group. It was nice to meet everyone the other day – almost therapeutic.

His next posting was entitled from 'Our correspondent in XXXX' and this was sent to the virtual café discussion thread (Box 5.9).

Box 5.9   Example posting

Greetings,

The idea of sitting in a café is thoroughly appealing, particularly in a dry country. In fact there is only one bar here and that is run for the British aid community here (I did, however, get myself invited to a party in the US marine compound the other night which was a laugh, but that's another story . . .).

One of the characteristics of being away is that you get time to think, and one of the comments from our f-2-f workshop has been exercising my mind. We were talking about what happens after this course, particularly if we are to form a group of mentors for a following group. I don't know if anyone else will know what I am talking about, but I am a member of an online community called H2G2. Originally set up by Douglas Adams it is an online version of *The Hitch Hiker's Guide to the Galaxy*, but is also a thriving community. Douglas Adams aside, could we develop our own online community along those lines?

> I don't know about anyone else, but I enjoy participating in this course, because I don't get strange looks when I post ideas, I enjoy discussing online learning in a positive context and I learn a lot just from being online. Also, in a way, this group is a form of 'therapy' away from those who are just not interested. It would be a shame to lose those things.
>
> If you are interested in having a look, you can access H2G2 through the BBC website and get a tour. You won't find my name because we all have 'nicknames', that is alter egos, and I'm not telling you mine!
>
> In the meantime I am going to drink this coke and dream of beer.
>
> Patrick

Humour can be a delicate balancing act but when it is part and parcel of a healthy, thriving community interaction it can really add to the sense of enjoyment of a group. Our advice would be to handle with care at all times. Beware of community pranksters. They can set up reactions just for the sake of setting up reactions. We have had a few experiences of this, for example in one community a member assumed a series of different identities just as a joke (it caused confusion, irritation and left the community feeling slightly bruised), in another community a member faked anger and pretended to be upset (to find out the impact of these emotions on a virtual community), resulting in an emotional maelstrom that took a week or so to settle down. These kinds of activities can be very dangerous and can have a very damaging impact on otherwise healthy communities. Some communities prefer to keep all light-hearted contributions within a virtual café or pub discussion forum. This is personal preference and will depend on the individuals within your groups.

Nurturing the four conditions

The following checklists (Table 5.2 and Table 5.3) may be used by facilitators and members to provide a framework for nurturing the four conditions of a healthy virtual community.

Summary

The incubation phase is an important phase in the life cycle of a learning community as the foundations of good practice are established and the conditions for healthy growth are embedded. During the incubation phase successful communities establish a safe and comfort-giving environment where honesty and trust are nurtured and cooperative and co-dependent ways of working are encouraged; a place where humour and fun are found.

Table 5.2 Checklist for facilitators

Conditions	*Possible actions*
Comfort zones	Encourage honesty and acknowledge feelings
	Assure members that confidentiality will be respected
	Give lots of positive feedback
	Use narratives during early phase to encourage sharing and disclosure
	Establish a members profiling area so that they can get to know each other's background
	Support those lacking in confidence
Commitment and trust	Model honesty
	Open debates on commitment
	Review needs of community regularly
	Follow up members who seem to lack commitment
	Model commitment
	Accept that some communities will founder due to lack of commitment and that it is not your sole responsibility
	Encourage co-dependency
Collective responsibility and co-dependency	Invite those with expertise to lead on identified activities
	Don't feel responsible for all community interactions
	Guide from the side and develop the knack of standing back
	Use questioning techniques and scaffold activities in such a way as to encourage participants to find their own answers
Humour	Encourage humour
	Initiate humour
	Don't stand on dignity
	Try to build in fun
	Beware pranksters – they can be saboteurs in jokers' clothing

Table 5.3 Checklist for members

Conditions	Possible checks
Comfort zones	Have I spent time online getting to know how to use the technical systems?
	Have I spent time online getting to know community members?
	Have I acknowledged and responded to other members' postings?
	Have I shared my feelings with the group?
	Have I shared my concerns and worries?
	Have I owned up to my own lack of knowledge or expertise in a particular area?
	Have I owned up to my own expertise?
	Am I comfortable? If not, why not?
	Do I have any suggestions for improvements?
	Am I prepared to take risks?
Commitment and trust	Have I committed time to the community?
	Am I committed to the purpose of the community?
	Am I honest in my contributions?
	Do I trust the other members? If not, why not?
Collective responsibility and co-dependency	Do I take responsibility for those areas of expertise that I could contribute to the community?
	Do I ask other members for help?
	Have I encouraged and supported other group members?
	Is the facilitator guiding from the side?
	What have I learnt from the facilitators' approach?
	Do I support other members?
Humour	Is the community fun?
	Whose sense of humour do I enjoy?
	Does any humour need challenging?
	Do we have pranksters?

6

The Community Life Cycle: Improving Performance, Implementation, Closure or Change Phases

Introduction

Once the virtual learning community is established through the induction and incubation phases then the stage is set for the community to move into improving performance and implementation. These are the stages when individual community members develop their knowledge and skills, and then start to apply them in the workplace. This is followed by the closure or change phase when the community either comes to the end of its natural life or metamorphoses into a new community.

In this chapter we will explore these three phases in the life cycle of the community and we will look in some detail at the role of the facilitator. Community facilitators are often involved in planning, designing and facilitating learning activities and this is explored with special reference to case studies, project work and virtual visitors in supporting the life and growth of the community. In addition we will look at the types of activities that are required to enable the community's passage through its life cycle leading to successful closure or transformation into a new community.

Phase 4 Improving performance

This is the phase when the serious business of the community starts to happen. Group members are likely to be working on real work-based problems and sharing resources and knowledge and understanding. The learning community is performing at its full potential as real-life issues are tackled and the members work collaboratively to develop practical solutions. The speed of work at this phase may be very fast with messages posted on a daily and sometimes hourly basis. Group members are likely to be engrossed in collaborative work practices and there is often a sense of excitement as individuals and the learning community are working on the boundaries of current practice.

This stage may include examples of:

- The whole group brainstorming, pooling ideas and resources.
- Developing, agreeing and implementing an action plan.
- Individuals testing out ideas and asking for feedback.
- Whole group synchronous discussions, for example face-to-face or in conference rooms.
- Production of draft ideas, reports and products.
- Creating new knowledge and understanding.
- Developing innovative work practices.
- Developing solutions to work-based problems.
- Production of new products and by-products.
- Collaborative project outcomes.

There is often a sense of hard work and a real commitment to achieving group goals. The group is likely to work constructively to share ideas, resources and solutions. There is likely to be evidence of the trust, openness and honesty, and good humour that have been established during the incubation phase. At this stage the group is going to be involved in both sharing and managing information and resources. They may be exchanging information based on their own knowledge and experiences, and there is often a real need for this information to be managed. This is particularly important in very active communities when large numbers of postings can lead to information overload. The provision of summaries, outline reports, action plans, etc. can all help to manage the information that is generated during the improving performance phase.

The role of the facilitator

The facilitator is likely to be less involved in the life of the community than in the previous stages. The learning community is now functioning as a community and the facilitator's role is likely to involve gentle steering and perhaps ensuring that the group keeps to task. The facilitator may introduce new ideas, act as a critical friend, and also provide feedback and support to the whole group. Once a community is established they may decide that the role of facilitator is no longer relevant to their needs, members take on more proactive roles and the purpose of the community provides enough commitment to carry the group forward to achieving their goal. This is illustrated in the example shown in Box 6.1.

The facilitator's role is likely to involve supporting and providing feedback to the community's ideas. Sometimes the facilitator may take on the role of critical friend and offer constructive ideas to enable the development of a workable solution. Increasingly the role of critical friend will be assumed by other members of the community and the facilitator needs to encourage this behaviour in community members.

Box 6.1   Example of collaborative writing within a learning community

---

One of the authors experienced this phase with a group of colleagues (who worked in different universities across the UK). They collaborated to produce an academic conference paper. This group emerged from a virtual learning community based around a Masters degree in Networked Collaborative Learning and the group called themselves the TLG group, that is they had moved beyond the existing community boundaries to establish a new community. From the initial idea through to the submission and acceptance of the paper the group worked at an extremely fast rate. Ideas were shared and problems tackled with vigour. The paper gradually grew as different members took responsibility for different aspects – literature review, data analysis, etc. The final product was generally accepted by the group as being a truly collaborative piece of work as it was impossible to identify who had written which part of the paper. In discussion the individual authors said that the final work demonstrated a creativity and breadth of ideas greater than that which might have been achieved by any of the individuals within the group. This whole process was carried out via a virtual learning environment and the group did not physically meet until the conference.

Planning, designing and facilitating learning activities

One of the important responsibilities of community facilitators at this stage is to design effective learning activities that mobilize, engage and enable learners to develop their knowledge and skills. Salmon (2000) discusses the concept of mobilization and this involves generating interest and motivation in taking part in community activities. Once learners are mobilized then they can engage with the learning process and this 'involves cognitive processes such as creating, problem-solving, reasoning, decision-making and evaluation' (Kearsley and Schneiderman 1998). Effective learning activities are those that enable groups or communities to work on authentic tasks or situations. The best type of learning activities are those that engage community members in real-life situations that they experience in or can relate to their own workplace. When designing such activities the facilitators will need to consider the following issues:

1. Purpose or aim of the task.
2. Learning outcomes or objectives (if this is appropriate).
3. Member numbers.
4. Overall structure of the task.

5. Interaction structure:
    – collaboration requirement (including deadlines);
    – process and outcome;
    – time required by community members.
6. Identification of resource requirements.

Table 6.1 summarizes commonly used community learning activities and tasks that can be used to encourage a community during the improving performance phase, it also highlights their advantages and potential problems.

Examples of activities used successfully during the improving performance phase

In the following section examples of three different learning activities are explored as a means of illustrating how community learning activities may be facilitated. The types of activity selected are case studies, project work and virtual visitors.

Case studies

Case studies are a useful method of enabling community members to focus on a particular situation and to explore it in depth and develop 'solutions'. They take some time to prepare as the facilitator needs to collect appropriate materials and examples, work out an appropriate case study, and then mentally 'walk through' the case study and the likely processes that the learners will engage in as they work on the materials. The best case studies are those based on real situations that are closely linked with the learners' experiences. The case study shown in Box 6.2 was successfully used with the Birmingham University e-learning community. While some of the learners expressed their surprise at the types of situations that were introduced into the case study, they were all based on recent experiences within a higher education institution.

This activity generated a lot of discussion and also research into the host organization's policies and procedures. Discussions focused around the following themes:

1. The need to prioritize and deal with the pornography issue and alleged harassment situation first.
2. The need to follow formal procedures, for example computer misuse, harassment and bullying procedures.
3. When to intervene or let matters resolve themselves.
4. When to intervene in discussion group or when a private response is more appropriate.
5. The need to differentiate between typographic errors and dyslexia, and the importance of diagnostic tools and support for individuals with special needs.
6. The need for e-tutors to have support and back-up from their institution.

Table 6.1 Learning activities that can be used to stimulate community activity during the improving performance phase

	Characteristics	Reasons for use	Advantages	Potential problems
Brainstorming or wordstorming	Individuals pool ideas and generate new ideas/ options. A 'quick' activity and therefore probably best carried out in a chat or conference room	Enables ideas and new perspectives to be identified. Useful for focusing learners on a new topic	Quick and simple method	Can be very time-consuming to develop. Individual learners may not engage with the activity
Case studies	Learners are presented with a particular situation and are typically asked to explore it and develop 'solutions'	Enables individuals to explore different situations from a range of different perspectives. Enables learners to share ideas and experiences, and construct new knowledge and understanding	Case studies can be closely related to workplace situations. Can be used to prepare learners for future situations	Can be very time-consuming to develop. May not be perceived as 'real' and therefore not valued. Individual learners may not engage with the activity
Debates	Structured or unstructured discussion based on two or more different perspectives	Enables learners to explore issues or ideas. Enables learners to share ideas and experiences, and construct their knowledge	The best debates are lively, based on real work-based issues and concerns. Involves all learners	Debate becomes a slanging match. Use of abusive language. A few members dominate. Quieter group members may feel intimidated
Discussion groups	Structured or unstructured discussions. May be based on a specific issue or set of ideas	Enables learners to explore issues or ideas. Enables learners to share ideas and experiences, and construct their knowledge	The best online discussions are lively, based on real work/ professional issues and concerns. Involves all learners	Discussion peters out or is unfocused. Learners don't participate or hijack discussion. Individuals dominate. They are not inclusive

Specific work-related tasks	Typically a facilitator sets up and facilitates exercises that involve pairs, trios or larger groups of community members working together on a specific task, e.g. produce a set of guidelines, review a website, produce a product	Enables learners to work in a focused way and benefit from sharing of experience, ideas and support within a tightly controlled timescale	Can be highly motivating and satisfying experiences. Individuals learn from each other. Products may be of higher quality than if produced by individuals	Time needs to be spent on working out how to work together.
Project groups	In cooperative groups individuals work on their own task and share ideas, feedback and give each other support. In collaborative groups the whole group works on a whole group project	Can be based on workplace projects. Enables multi-disciplinary or multi-professional teams to work together. Helps to develop team working and virtual communication skills. Encourages sharing of experience, ideas and support	Can be highly motivating and satisfying experiences. Individuals learn from each other. Products may be of higher quality than if produced by individuals	Time needs to be spent on working out how to work together. Individuals may opt out
Simulations or games	A group follows a set of rules or a situation that simulates a real-life situation. May be facilitated by a facilitator or group member(s)	Enables individuals to experience a 'real-life' situation. May provide experiences that are hard to work on in real life	Provides practical experience in handling particular situations. Time to reflect and learn from experiences	Can be very time-consuming to develop. May not be perceived as 'real' and therefore not valued. May be difficult to relate experiences to workplace

Continued

Table 6.1 continued

	Characteristics	Reasons for use	Advantages	Potential problems
Team building activities	A group takes part in an activity that involves everyone (the online equivalent to outward bound training). The discussion and reflection on the activity is more important than the actual activity itself	Enables community members to experience and become familiar with online group work	Learners can develop online netiquette skills and gain experience of good practice in team work	Individuals don't engage with activity and may perceive it as a waste of time. Learners don't participate or individuals dominate
Virtual visitor or guest speaker	Typically a facilitator invites an experienced practitioner or someone with specialist expertise to visit online community either synchronously or asynchronously for a set period of time	Introduces specialist knowledge. Opportunity to explore different perspectives. May be used to emphasize particular perspective	'Breath of fresh air'. Provides 'excitement' and 'difference'. Provides additional ideas, experiences, perspectives	Technical issues, for example problems with access to site. Virtual visitor doesn't prepare for visit and misreads culture or tone of group. Virtual visitor 'hijacks' session and leads it into an unwanted arena. Virtual visitor usurps facilitator's role. Learners don't engage with activity and 'ignore' visitor. Learners don't accept virtual visitor. Unrealistic expectations (facilitator, virtual visitor or learners)

| Virtual visits | A group of e-learners may visit another group and share their experiences using chat or discussion groups | Opportunity to explore different perspectives | 'Breath of fresh air'. Provides 'excitement' and 'difference'. Provides additional ideas, experiences, perspectives | Time needed to set up and organize visit. Technical issues, for example, problems with access to site. Problems with different groups of learners developing rapport. Visit becomes a social rather than a learning experience. Unrealistic expectations (facilitator, virtual visitor or learners) |

Box 6.2   Example case study: Working with diverse groups

Aim

The aim of this activity is to enable you to explore issues about working with diverse groups of learners online.

What you will need to do

1. Read the guide to online tutoring. This will provide you with an overview of the role of an e-tutor.
2. Working in your teams explore and discuss the case study. Some questions to prompt discussion are included at the end of the case study.
3. The e-learning group in the case study is clearly not working well. What actions would you take as their e-facilitator to resolve some of the issues identified in the case study? What type of learning activity would you introduce to get the group working together? How would you take into account the individual differences portrayed in the case study?
4. As a result of your work each team needs to produce a set of guidelines on working with diverse groups. These guidelines will be used for a training programme for new e-facilitators.
5. Please present your results to the whole group by 11 March.

Case study

Two of you have been asked to take over an e-learning group (12 members) at very short notice as the group's two e-facilitators have both gained promotion and moved to new pastures. The two e-facilitators took a team approach to the group: one offered expertise in IT and the internet (she is based in Information and Library Services) while the other offers subject expertise. The e-learning group (NewSkills Group) is a 40-week-long programme and it enables members to develop their IT, communication and online skills in the context of a specific subject. It is a Level 1 programme.

Information obtained from WebCT discussion group and e-mail

You begin exploring the group discussion forum and discover that there is a wide range of issues in the group that need tackling. As you read through the messages you print out significant ones and make your own notes. Here are your findings:

Janet

Although the group is now six weeks old Janet appears to have read less than a third of the messages. She has posted 10 messages (most group members have posted between 50 and 100) and these are all very short and supportive of other people's work. She hasn't contributed new ideas or helped develop discussions within her small groupwork project.

Hello everyone,
I agree with all the comments made by John and Susan. I'm still not clear about what we have to produce as a group report. Does anyone know?
Janet

Terry

Terry is a very active group member. She appears to log on every few hours. Terry tends to answer everyone's queries and has strong opinions. She caused an upset with the following messages:

Hi everyone
Time is short! Would everyone make sure they put the right subject heading on their messages. It is netiquette and helps me to file everything away.
Thanks.
Terry

Hi everyone
I've read the documents and understand the task. I suggest that James and Andy do the research, I'll collate their findings and write the first draft. Jane could edit it and make sure I don't make any typos. I think this is the best way of going forward. It builds on our strengths. (I won't mention what happened in the first activity.) When will you produce the first draft J and A?
Terry

James

James appears to be progressing well. He is online three or four times a week and works well in a group. His messages are always very supportive.

Andrew

Andrew has only posted a few messages. They are very short and you are concerned about his literacy skills. Is he dyslexic?

Hi
OK about reading. Will search for more dotumets. Im confused about activiuy help
Andy

Susanne

As you are working through the site an e-mail arrives from one of the students, Susanne.

Hello,
I understand you are the two new tutors for the NewSkills Group. I am very unhappy about the group. I contacted the old tutors (by e-mail) and they seemed to ignore me. I am being bullied by two of the women. They ignore me, patronize me and put me down (read the messages and you'll find this is true). One of them thinks she is better than me and offered to teach me how to use WebCT – she sent me three e-mails to my home address offering help. Is she a stalker? Can you sort them out. I don't want to work in a group with them. Will you throw them off the course? Otherwise I'll use the university's equal opportunities policy and take you all to court. You have three days to reply to this e-mail.
Suzanne

Jane

Jane appears to be working well on the programme. You are concerned about her workload as she has posted a number of messages that suggest she is stressed out. Unfortunately there has been no response to these messages. Here is an example message posted at 1.05 am.

Hi
Sorry this is late. Working til 10 pm again last night. My cat died this morning too. Back to work now.
Jane

Adrian

Adrian seems to be hanging around the edge of the group. He reads messages but rarely inputs anything of value to the group activities. Terry called him a 'free-loader' when she worked with him. He ignored her comment. Adrian has suggested that group members visit his personal website so that they can see how 'a good website is designed'. You visit it and, to your horror, discover that it contains pornographic material. You are sickened by the images you see. You wonder if other students have visited it. There is no mention of it in the discussion group.

Anne

Anne appears to be working through the programme with ease. Her messages are friendly and supportive. She often gives help and support to others.

Sam

Sam only logs on once a week as he can only access WebCT at the weekend. He does contribute a lot during the weekend but often seems to be out of step with the groupwork. He is obviously doing a lot of reading and thinking. His contributions are really high quality.

Russell

Russell is an active member of the group and often helps to get the team work moving forward. He is obviously technically very skilled but is careful not to use jargon or introduce ideas that are very much in advance of the course. He has given a lot of his time to help others overcome technical issues.

Elizabeth

Elizabeth is concerned about the amount of work involved in the course and also the cost of being online. This is her latest message:

Hi
I am getting fed up with this course. There are too many messages to read and a lot of them are about social chit chat rather than the WORK. I came on the course to get a qualification and learn more about IT. I dind't come here to make new friends (I've got enough friends anyway and I hardly have time to see them). Could everyone cut out the chat and get on with the work.
Liz

Victoria

Vicky is struggling to keep up with the reading but is fully involved in all the team activities. She is really good at supporting others and often brings a 'down to earth' approach to the work. She uses a lot of appropriate humour in her team work.

Prompt questions

Having read the messages you need to explore and discuss your findings within your group. Here are some prompt questions to start off the process:

1. How can the e-tutors sort this out?
2. That porn site was revolting. Isn't there a policy about offensive materials within the university? Should the e-tutors report it to the police? Should the e-tutors discuss it with a colleague? What issues are involved in this situation?
3. How could the e-tutors handle the alleged bullying situation?
4. What other issues are present in the group? How could they be handled?

5. What issues will the e-tutors handle? What issues will they leave to the group to handle?
6. How could the e-tutors keep this group working together?

The guidelines produced by the community members enabled them to summarize their fndings and it provided them with a useful tool for use in their information service.

Project work

Community members are often working on projects in the workplace and these may also be worked on in the learning community. Problem-solving projects are popular and important as they enable participants to share ideas and expertise and perhaps develop innovative solutions to problems. Community members may share and work on a common problem or they may take turns in working together on a colleague's workplace problem. Examples of project work are shown in Box 6.3 and Box 6.4.

Box 6.3   Example: Collaborative project work

The following activity was used with managers of an organization offering support services to the steel industry. A group of middle managers participating in a virtual learning community identified a reluctance to use ICT within their employing organization. Computers and internet connections were available in the workplace but many of the employees including senior managers did not make use of them, not even for e-mail. They discussed this situation with the facilitator and the facilitator designed an activity requiring them to demonstrate the value of ICT by encouraging the managers to use ICT to provide a solution to a work-based problem.

The following activity was devised by the facilitators to initiate the process:

Activity 2. Design a solution using learning technologies to a work-based problem

The aim of this activity is to encourage participants to use learning technologies to produce a solution to an identified work-based problem.

What you should do

Working in your groups you need to identify a real work-based opportunity for using learning technologies to improve performance or services in your organization, please base your plan on using the technical infrastructure already available in your organization. You will need to design and outline a project plan. This will involve thinking about and answering many of the following questions. Summarize your answers to the questions in a Word document:

1. Why is there a need to develop this solution?
2. Why is there a need to deliver it using learning technologies?
3. How will the proposed project meet the aims and objectives of your company?
4. How would the proposed activity serve the needs of your work-based teams/organization?
5. Who are the potential users – numbers, their background, ICT background, entry knowledge and skills?
6. How would the use of ICT meet the needs of your customers and colleagues?
7. What are the draft aims and outcomes of the project?
8. What is the type of structure you have in mind? Will it involve training? Will you need to produce interactive training materials, a structured training programme involving identified groups and/or a blended approach of face-to-face and online training?
9. Give a brief description of the type of project you have in mind.
10. Is there a budget? And if so then what is it?
11. Who will be working on this project?
12. How much time have you got? Work out a rough figure for the next 2–6 months.

You will then need to produce a project outline. This will be supported by a summary of your responses to the previous questions.

Post these two documents by 5 June in the Blackboard site.

Box 6.4   Example: Project management e-learning course for information workers

---

During 2003 Barbara ran a learning community on project management for library and information workers and this involved a blended mix of face-to-face and virtual workshops. Cooperative groups were set up in which members worked in small groups on their own workplace projects. They used standard project management tools, for example MS Project and gained help, support and encouragement from each other as well as their facilitator. The types of projects that members worked on included:

- Implementation of a new integrated information system.
- Development of a digital learning resource centre.
- Development of a departmental website.

- Production of a new set of printed resources.
- Closure of a learning resource centre.

Overall, the members achieved the following outcomes:

- They learnt standard project management skills and techniques.
- They applied their new knowledge and skills to workplace information projects.
- They developed new virtual communication skills.
- They internalized the experiences of an e-learner.
- They developed as a learning community that continued after the end of the course.

Virtual visitors

Virtual visitors are sometimes invited as special guests to a learning community: they may be individuals or practitioners with particular experiences or expertise, for example: a community of nurses were exploring issues around supporting patients with a particular disability and as part of their online learning community they invited a teenage patient and their parent to visit a synchronous chat session to share their experiences as patient and parent. This stimulated an animated discussion and the learning community continued to explore many of the issues raised later in the asynchronous discussion forum. The visiting patient also reported that he had enjoyed the experience and had found that he had more to say than he realized.

However, importing outsiders into closely gelled communities can create tensions, particularly if there is a clash of learning modes. We invited an international 'expert' in e-learning to visit one of our e-learning communities to discuss his most recent publication in an asynchronous discussion forum over a period of two weeks. The 'expert' supplied an electronic copy of his paper before the visit and the participants had familiarized themselves with the content before he entered into an extended discussion. Evaluations of this experience later revealed that participants had reservations about the success of this 'visit' . . . The learning community had established a close collaborative working relationship with each other and also with us as their facilitators. The visitor created a new dynamic and some participants felt that it seemed like an intrusion. We had been 'guiding from the side' and nurturing collaborative approaches to learning within the community then suddenly a 'sage on the stage' was imported into the learning environment and it created tensions.

As with face-to-face encounters the organization of virtual visits involves a fair amount of preparation and administration. In particular, the organization of synchronous sessions can be particularly demanding and stressful as they depend on everyone having access to a working virtual environment at the same time. Guidelines such as those shown in Box 6.5 may be used to help organize and support virtual visits.

Box 6.5   Example: Guidelines for virtual visits

Guidelines for virtual speakers

- Clarify aims, outcomes and expectations of visit.
- Prepare for visit, for example read course documents, read previous discussions, read member biographies, discuss purpose of visit and expectations with tutor(s).
- Minimize introduction of additional reading materials.
- Provide a photo of yourself.
- Provide links to websites etc. that you have been involved in.
- Provide any reading materials in advance.
- Introduce self and clarify expectations, for example how often you will log into discussion, total length of time you will be online.
- Spend some time establishing rapport, for example acknowledge comments made by learners, make connections with their work, earlier stages of programme.
- Focus discussion on an authentic situation or activity.
- Include time for closure and say 'goodbye'.

Guidelines for facilitators

- Make contact with virtual visitor several weeks before visit.
- Negotiate fees and expenses.
- Clarify aims, outcomes and expectations of visit.
- Ensure that virtual visitor's contribution to the online group is timely.
- Provide visitor with guidelines.
- Provide learners with background information and photo of visitor.
- Provide learners with aims, outcomes and expectations of visit.
- Integrate visit with learning activities – make it an integral part of the course and, ideally, link it with assessment activities.
- Introduce visitor in the discussion group, keep a low profile.
- Thank the visitor in discussion group and also by private e-mail.

Guidelines for community members

- Identify aim, learning outcomes and expectations of visit.
- Identify what you can gain from visit.
- Prepare a list of questions you want to discuss with visitor.
- Read introductory material including visitor biography.
- Welcome visitor and help them to obtain a 'quick snapshot' of you.
- Participate in discussions and be supportive of visitor.
- Thank visitor at end.

Phase 5   Implementation

The purpose of most work-based learning communities is to support improvement practices in the workplace; communities that are successful lead to improvements in the workplace and changes to the participants' professional identities. The implementation phase involves transferring learning from the community to the work situation. This can be in the form of a product or outcome or it can be in the form of changed work practices, for example implementation of personal transferable skills and practitioner expertise. Some communities work towards implementing a single project or improvement practice, whereas other communities have a much more strategic and dispersed impact on the workplace.

Implementing a single project or output from a community activity

Learning communities that are formed to focus on specific projects are likely to rely on a member with project management knowledge and skills to implement the outcomes of the community activity. The project manager will need to carry out the following types of activities:

- identifying how the project will be managed and supported;
- planning the implementation process (who does what, when and how);
- identifying the resources (people, financial and other resources);
- developing and implementing a communication strategy;
- implementing the plan;
- reviewing and evaluating the change and also the process of change.

In this situation the learning community will often provide an invaluable source of support, ideas and feedback for the community member who has taken up the role of project manager. If the learning community is established within an employing organization then it may take on the role of project team or this role may be delegated to operational staff. In this situation the learning community may act as a steering group and/or as a source of mentoring for the project manager.

This stage also involves knowledge management and transfer. The knowledge developed within the learning community will need to be explicitly identified and then transferred to the relevant people within the organization or profession. In some communities the responsibility for this process is carried by an individual member who may be a qualified information or knowledge worker and a member of an association such as the Chartered Institute for Library and Information Professionals (CILIP) or ASLIB/IMI. Their role is to select, organize and present the knowledge in an appropriate manner, for example reports and databases using tools such as intranets and the internet. In addition they may need to start work on ensuring the intellectual capital is owned by the organization, for example through copyright, trademark or patents.

At this stage the facilitator's role is likely to involve supporting and providing feedback to the group's ideas; this will include validating and confirming their achievements. In addition the facilitator may take on an additional role to ensure that the product or outcome is implemented within the organization or professional group.

Implementing complex programmes of change

As discussed in Chapter 2 some communities are formed as a strategic response to the need for the workforce development of a particular region or organization. These communities are often complex and the implementation of their outcomes can be diverse and wide-ranging.

University of Birmingham

As a result of participating in the Birmingham University learning community academics, information services staff and ICT trainers developed new working practices. Each of the community members implemented changes within their professional area, for example the law academic used WebCT to provide a virtual learning experience for incipient law students. All new students are now provided with access to WebCT before the beginning of term and they are invited to participate in discussions that will be developed further during the first term. The outcomes of the learning community have also impacted on their working practices across the university; multi-professional teams were formed to work on the development of new programmes, for the first time ICT staff and librarians worked with academics and had an input into the creation of the learning environment for academic study programmes.

Management of change in a public sector organization

A large department in a public sector organization was undergoing a restructuring which was managed by a 'change team' made up of senior and middle managers. As part of the change process the team established a virtual communications site where staff could ask questions and comment on the change process. This site was extremely active and on some days there were 50+ hits. Individual members of staff used the site to comment on the proposed changes, vent their feelings and also ask specific questions of their managers. A core group of 22 (out of 76 staff) were active on the site. The site was facilitated by a member of the change team and part of his role involved directing questions or comments to individual managers or the director for them to respond to. In addition to activities on the site it was often referred to in team meetings and also informal communications where typically staff would comment on questions and the responses to them. Once the new structure came into place then the site was closed down. An evaluation of the site indicated that it provided a useful vehicle for the exchange of feedback on the change process and also it enabled all staff to have equal access to the new plans, ideas and related discussions. It was particularly popular with part-time staff, one of whom said 'I learnt more about the proposed changes from the ChangeSite than official documents or meetings. I didn't send any questions in but reading other people's and also the answers kept me up-to-date on the key issues, it should be repeated for future changes/projects.'

In this example the process of engaging with management of change issues in the virtual community resulted in staff becoming more able to cope with the change process. In the life cycle of the community the implementation phase is not always about producing products or hard outputs, it can be about working more effectively and being more reconciled to the work situation.

Phase 6 Closure or change

The learning community may come to the end of its natural life, for example as a result of achieving its initial goals and this may result in community closure or it may evolve into a new community with a new goal. If the learning community closes then it may go through the traditional rituals of closure, for example reflection on the life of the learning community, celebration of achievements, party (face-to-face or virtual), exchange of personal contact details. These enable the community and its members to complete their business and say their 'goodbyes'.

At this stage the facilitator may be required to become more active than during the previous improving performance and implementation phases. The facilitator may be involved in initiating and supporting closure activities; or in helping members move to a new community. In one learning community facilitated by the authors the community had come to the end of its life cycle, that is, it had achieved its goals, and members indicated that they wanted the community to continue. Agreement was made to e-mail all community members after four weeks to re-establish the community but when the time came there were no replies to this e-mail, the community had closed and individual members had moved on to new activities.

If the learning community evolves into a new community then it will start the life cycle again with the initiation process. This may be extremely brief and take place over a few days as members discuss the 'new community' and re-establish themselves with a new goal and direction. Alternatively it may involve a series of discussions and negotiations with the employing organization. The new community may involve different members, for example a mixture of people from the 'old' community and also new members. In this type of situation the induction and incubation periods are vitally important if the 'new' community is to work effectively and not break down into a series of cliques. The facilitator is likely to be very active in the establishment of the new community and supporting it through the community life cycle.

The ending of a virtual learning community needs careful management to make sure that a variety of processes take place. It is important to ensure that the learning process is consolidated and members often find it helpful to spend time reflecting on their development process. The group process needs to be completed and this often involves reflecting on the life of the community, celebrating strengths and successes, acknowledging weaknesses, and discussing the end of the community and the need for individuals to leave and move onto the next stage. In some organizations the transactions and transcripts produced by the community will be harvested as new knowledge and archived. During the closure stage the community is likely to be evaluated and this is considered in the final chapter. It is up to the facilitator to ensure that community members have a sense of reaching an ending and they have no unfinished business and that there is time to complete the closure process in an unhurried way (Box 6.6).

Box 6.6   Facilitator activities for closing a virtual learning community

- Signal the forthcoming end of the community.
- Give members time, for example up to four weeks in a community with a long life span, to engage with the closure process.
- Introduce an activity that enables members to reflect on their community experiences, the high spots and the low spots, and their achievements.
- Share your own experiences as a facilitator and ask for feedback.
- Introduce an activity to evaluate the virtual learning community and its achievements (see Chapter 11).
- Ask individuals to produce an action plan.
- Arrange a farewell meal or equivalent virtual get together.
- Remember to actually say 'goodbye' and inform everyone of your final visit to the community.

Birmingham e-learning community

In this community the end was signalled by the two facilitators several weeks before the community finally closed. Part of the closure process included an evaluation of the community and its achievements and, in addition, we met up with as many members as possible for a farewell lunch. This proved to be a success with members and facilitators sharing their stories about their individual virtual journey. Almost two years after the closure of the community a smaller group of members met up with facilitators and this provided an opportunity to share news and discuss the impact of the community on their working lives.

Table 6.2 Summary of the virtual learning community life cycle

	Foundation	Induction	Incubation	Improving performance	Implementation	Closure or change
Key features	Framework for learning community is established. Infrastructure including ICT is set up	Individuals join the learning community and are introduced to it	Social activity. Creation of comfort zones. Encourage co-dependency. Honesty, trust, humour, fun	Starts work on real-life problems. Collaborative and cooperative work. Leaning activities designed to improve work-based practice. Development and testing of new practice/products. Feedback	Transfer of ideas and practice into the workplace.	Learning community no longer required and is closed. Learning community may fizzle out or it transforms itself into another learning community with different focus/membership
Facilitator's levels of activity	Very active	Very active	Very active	Guiding from the side and moving towards periphery	On periphery	Facilitates closure or the initiation of a new learning community

Facilitator activities	Gain agreement from senior management. Establish infrastructure. Ensure appropriate ICT support is available. Identify potential aims and goals of community. Identify potential members	If appropriate organize and run face-to-face event. Welcome everyone to community. Negotiate ground rules. Build trust and confidence in community. Make contact with non-participants. Ensure everyone has access	Inject confidence about practice. Inject ideas. Encourage honesty and trust. Set up social areas. Set activities that encourage members to 'open up'	Designs learning activities and community challenges. Provides structure and support. Makes links with theory, practice and workplace. Support and feedback	Involved in feedback and support. Focus is on practice and sharing good practice. May be involved in project management process	Facilitates closure, e.g. review, goodbyes. Facilitates arrangements to move forward into initiation stage.
Threats	ICT challenges. Appropriate people not getting involved	Lack of trust. Limited or no access. Time. Working outside comfort zone. Commitment to purpose	Social conflict. Personality clashes. Time. Comfort zone. Commitment to purpose. Lack of honesty	Group dynamics. Low participation. Information overload. Insider/outsider. Saboteurs. Sub-groups. Distractions	Don't take responsibility for outcomes. Lack of transfer. Fear of change	Group stuck. Don't want to move forward. Ends abruptly without closure
Information and knowledge management	Creating information infrastructure	Information transmission	Information shared and exchanged	Information management. Collaborative approaches to developing new knowledge	Knowledge management. Knowledge transfer	Information transmission and exchange. Archiving

TLG Group

This community formally came to an end after members had met up at a conference and presented their collaborative paper. During the conference the members met up for lunch which proved to be an interesting and hilarious event as we found that we were all talking at the same time and seemed to have lost the ability to converse outside of a discussion group forum. After the conference members moved back into the main group and became full participants in that group again. A few members of the group still keep in contact via e-mail.

Summary

Virtual learning communities are likely to experience a developmental life cycle and the role of the facilitator is to support the community through this process. This is summarized in Table 6.2.

7

Community Participation

Introduction

The purpose of this chapter is to explore how individuals may contribute effectively to learning community development and activities. This is considered from the perspectives of community members and facilitators. It covers the following topics:

- roles and responsibilities;
- skills and attributes of effective members;
- group and team dynamics;
- working with co-facilitators;
- community participation levels.

Skills and attributes of effective members

A learning community needs a group of active and committed people to enable it to work. A minimum of four or five members is required to provide the type of diversity of ideas and experience that will enable people to learn through collaboration. We have found 6 to 16 participants to be the ideal number for an effective learning community. This allows for some discussions or activities to take place between sub-groups of participants and some activities and discussions to take place as a whole community. Mixing groups and encouraging participants to work in different combinations seems to work well and maximize creative collaboration.

Effective members are likely to be individuals who are committed to their membership of the learning community and who take an active role in the community activities. Effective members are likely to be people who:

- manage their time (see Chapter 9);
- develop skills in reading and following threads;
- develop an online voice;

- actively participate in community learning activities; and
- adopt different roles and responsibilities.

Managing time

Members cannot participate in the life and work of a community unless they manage their time effectively and participants report that taking part in asynchronous discussions involves them in developing different approaches to time. Many participants also talk of the misconception that many employers have of online learning; it is assumed that it is likely to take less time than face-to-face collaboration and many employers expect their employees to participate in online communities in their own time. There are so many issues associated with managing time in virtual learning communities that we have dedicated Chapter 9 to exploring them further.

Developing skills in reading and following threads

Membership of a virtual community involves reading many textual messages; over the life of a community there may be thousands of messages to read. Sometimes participants feel overwhelmed by the number of messages that they need to read. In lively groups or conferences someone may return from a few days holiday and be faced with 100+ messages. The pie chart Figure 7.1 illustrates the balance between asynchronous and synchronous activities in a very enthusiastic and committed community. The site had been hit over 2000

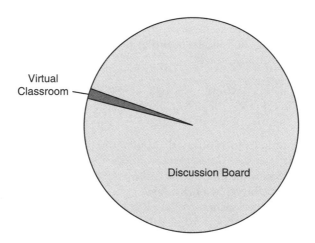

Total number of accesses: Discussion Board = 2752   98%
Total number of accesses: Virtual Classroom = 41   0.2%

Figure 7.1   Pie chart illustrating online activities in an enthusiastic group

times during the first four weeks of the community's life. This means that participants need to develop skills in using the electronic facilities within the VLE to help manage and sort messages. These vary according to the technical specification of the VLE but many have facilities to expand and collapse messages within threaded themed topics, and flags to indicate unread messages and search facilities.

In addition to developing skills in using the technical facilities, participants also need skills in skim reading and identifying key messages, analysing relatively large amounts of information and then synthesizing a number of different ideas and perspectives (this particular skill is called weaving). Many people find it easier to do this if they keep up-to-date with the messages and print out key messages. Online summaries, for example from the facilitator or a volunteer within the community, are a useful means of managing the information contained in messages (Box 7.1).

Box 7.1   Example of facilitator summary

Please find attached a summary of the characteristics that have been discussed in response to your paired activity identifying the characteristics of positive learning experiences. You can access attachments by clicking on the attachments title above this message frame. I hope that you will agree that we have generated a really useful list. I suggest that you reflect on this list and comment on it in your reflective log.

Characteristics of positive learning experiences

Here is an attempt to summarize the key points from Activity 4. Apologies for reducing ideas down to bullet points but I'm aiming for a quick overview of your key points:

Positive learning experiences are often about self-realization, real 'lightbulb' moments stick. Not about being taught facts and figures. Tutors/facilitators play a vital part. Good tutors/facilitators should:

- be well prepared, motivated, approachable, supportive and good listeners;
- take pride in what they do and enjoy it;
- know their subject, be enthusiastic;
- make sure their learners are at ease;
- keeping the learners focused should they veer off track;
- they need to be good observers;
- have the ability to give constructive and positive feedback – patience;
- know their audience and tailor the delivery to the participants.

The actual learning environment contributes towards a positive or negative learning experience, for example:

- a good location (parking, etc.), welcoming;
- the room layout can create barriers or contribute positively to inter-actions within a group;
- being too cold or too hot can affect one's concentration and if the room is dirty or littered with rubbish it makes me feel uneasy;
- when refreshments/drinks are available during training sessions it can make a difference;
- interruptions during learning can also be a distraction, for example mobile phones or people interrupting the tutor from outside the class.

Sometimes these factors are beyond the tutor's control but arriving before the students and welcoming each in a positive way can cheer up the location.

Tutors need to be aware of student worries. If a student is not able to be completely focused on the learning due to thinking or worrying about a personal concern then the experience will not be as positive as it could be.

As you can see, your comments fall into two main themes: the import-ance of the skills of the facilitator and also the importance of the environment. Your comments are focused on the physical environ-ment. As our experience in this online learning community develops, I think we should also bear in mind the importance of the virtual learn-ing environment. Which facilities and structures do you think really support positive learning online? How could this environment be improved to support more positive learning experiences? We'll return to this theme later in the programme.

Developing an online voice

Communicating and working together online is a new experience for many people. Most of us are experienced in communicating together in a face-to-face situation and have learnt how to project ourselves and our identity, but new entrants to virtual communities often find online communication a disorienting experience, they may become lost or confused in their attempts to communicate with invisible people using written messages without the reassurance of non-verbal feedback.

I miss the f2f aspect and look forward to the next f2f workshop . . . Confidence is a difficult one though. Being in this alien environment is off-putting enough but the fact that everything you say is there in black and white for all to see is daunting. I'm getting better as I'm receiving lots of positive responses to things I've said.

Brenda Birmingham

This emphasizes why the induction and incubation stages of the community life cycle are so important – they give community members the opportunity to develop a virtual identity. Developing a virtual identity involves learning to develop an appropriate tone and style in online communications, and learning to interpret the messages of others without the benefit of non-verbal signals and clues. It usually takes time to develop confidence in communicating and socializing online; it takes time to develop an online voice that is genuine and individual to us. However, there are some guidelines in online communication practice, often called 'netiquette', that are generally regarded as good practice and might be valuable to participants during the early phases. These are outlined in Box 7.2.

Box 7.2   Guide to netiquette

1. Thank, acknowledge and support others freely.
2. Acknowledge before differing.
3. Speak from your own perspective.
4. Avoid flaming spirals, that is losing your temper and sending off a series of replies in the heat of the moment.
5. Use emoticons to represent feelings, for example ☺, **grin**.
6. CAPITAL letters are the equivalent to shouting – use them sparingly.
7. Be cautious when quoting from other messages – don't over-quote as this leads to very long messages.
8. Be careful to send messages to the appropriate forum and thread – everyone makes mistakes at first but discussions will become very confused if messages are not sent to the appropriate thread.
9. Keep messages short. Longer messages need to be used as an attachment so people can choose to read them at leisure.
10. Don't respond to a message if you are experiencing strong negative feelings. Give yourself time to cool down.

As facilitators of virtual communities it may be useful to refer participants to the conventions of netiquette in the early stages of the life of a community.

Actively participate in community learning activities

Effective learning communities are likely to include members who are active learners and are constantly linking theory and practice, and striving to improve their work-based and professional practice. These people are likely to:

- be involved in a wide range of professional activities such as product development, service improvement, conference presentations and consultancy;
- keep up-to-date by reading current literature;
- network and discuss ideas with colleagues (both face-to-face and through virtual communications);
- be committed to their own and their colleagues' continuing professional development (CPD);
- be constantly looking for ways of improving their professional practice.

Membership of a learning community can enable a relative newcomer to a profession or project to become an active learner. Access to discussions, new ideas and good-quality resources can be highly motivating and can enable individuals to become more actively involved in their continuous professional development.

Becoming a lifelong learner
Susan was a member of one of our virtual learning communities and her initial role in this mirrored that of her full-time job as an administrator. As the learning community developed she became an extremely active participant and her confidence and self-esteem developed rapidly. Immediately after completing the community experience she enrolled on an Open University course in e-learning and successfully completed that course. This success gave her the confidence to apply for and obtain a place on a part-time degree programme. Susan was recently promoted and is now managing a team of administrators in an extremely challenging enterprise office. In a recent follow-up evaluation she acknowledged the positive effect that the help and support of the community had on her personal development and stated that her continuing professional development had been a direct result of the confidence that she developed in the virtual learning community.

Group and team dynamics

Successful participation in a learning community requires that participants take responsibility for their community and this may involve them in adopting different roles and responsibilities. In addition to functional roles, for example facilitator(s), administrators, technical support, community members are also likely to take on team roles and responsibilities. There are a wide variety of different theoretical models on team roles, we have used various models with different learning community groups. The following example (MEd 2000 Collaborative Group) demonstrates how the model developed by Meredith Belbin was used to encourage a learning community to reflect on group dynamics and to raise their awareness of their community interactions. His model has the advantages of being: widely used and accepted; simple; readily understood; and it provides a diagnostic tool.

Belbin identified nine team roles and these are outlined in Table 7.1. He suggests that teams made up of people who display these roles are more likely to be effective than teams made up of people who take on a limited number of roles. It is worth highlighting that Belbin's work related to traditional teams working face-to-face rather than to virtual learning communities.

Table 7.1 Belbin team roles

Type	Typical features	Positive qualities	Allowable weaknesses
Worker	Hard-working Conservative Predictable	Organizing ability, practical common sense, hard-working, self-discipline	May not be very flexible May be unresponsive to unproven ideas
Chair or coordinator	Self-confident Assertive High levels of emotional intelligence	Well organized Manages people Manages difficult situations Remains focused on outcomes	May not be highly creative
Shaper	Energetic Extrovert Dynamic	Drive Challenges *status quo*	Impatient Irritable
Plant	Individualistic Unorthodox	Imaginative Creative Thinks 'outside the box' Entrepreneur	'Head in the clouds' Ignores procedures Doesn't pay attention to detail
Resource investigator	Extrovert Enthusiastic Excellent communication skills	Maintains a wide network of friends and associates Enjoys a challenge Enthusiastic	Loses interest
Monitor evaluator	Serious Sensible Unemotional	Keeps focused on task and quality of work Checks progress against plan	May appear negative May de-motivate others
Team worker	Sociable Sensitive People-focused	Responds to individuals and supports them Helps to provide social 'glue' in group	May find it difficult to make challenging decisions
Completer finisher	Conscientious Methodical Well organized Orderly	Focuses on detail Checks all outcomes are achieved	May worry about details Gets things out of perspective
Specialist	Focused on own specialism	High level of knowledge and skills in a specific area	May only be able to contribute in own field

Med 2000 Collaborative Group

This example relates to a learning community that came together as part of a professional development programme. Seven community members from different education sectors (higher education, secondary education, further education and private training providers) worked together over two months on a project where they explored the use of virtual communication software as a means of supporting and enabling professional development. Barbara was a member of this group. Each member of the community completed the Belbin questionnaire and answered the following questions:

1. Does this model help clarify the roles I have taken in the community?
2. Does this model help clarify the roles other people have taken in the community?
3. Are there any gaps or unexplained roles occurring in the community?

An analysis of the postings in the discussion group supported the findings from the inventory, for example John, who scored most highly as completer finisher, showed a pattern of regular activity until towards the end of one of the communities' self-imposed deadlines when he appeared to 'spring into action' and worked hard to ensure that the group met its deadlines. No one in the group scored highly as coordinator and this was indicated by the fact that different individuals took on this role at different stages in the group. It was possible to use Belbin's model to illustrate and explore the roles we took in the group and this model provided a helpful framework for reflection and discussion. The group discussed the limitations of using this type of model, for example:

> My feeling is that the roles people played in this group are much more complex and fluid than can be described within the Belbin framework, or perhaps, within any such framework.

> In a process where one gets to genuinely like and admire a colleague, one is very reluctant to describe that person as a Worker, Chairs or Team Worker when such descriptions may carry some negative connotations.

In summary, in this learning community the Belbin framework provided a convenient way of identifying and clarifying the diversity of roles within the group. However, the model doesn't appear sufficient to describe and explain the complexity of behaviour that members displayed and one person suggested 'in a model describing the community teamwork, I would expect to see words such as support, understanding, negotiation, adaptability, flexibility. . . .' The demands of working in a community in a virtual learning environment using both asynchronous and synchronous communications meant that members took on a variety of roles with great flexibility in order to support the group and also complete the task (see Box 7.3).

Box 7.3   Summary of participant responsibilities

- Active regular participation
- Sharing expertise
- Sharing experience
- Sharing technical ability
- Committing to group ground rules
- Committing to achieve agreed activities and outcomes
- Being prepared to adopt a variety of roles

Facilitator(s)

The role of the facilitator is to support the community process, to design and support collaborative learning opportunities and also to facilitate the transfer of knowledge into professional practice. There may be a 'formal' facilitator who has been identified by the community's sponsor or the role of facilitator may have evolved organically within the community as one or more individuals carry out these activities. The facilitator may also be a trainer/tutor with an identified responsibility for planning learning activities and defining learning outcomes.

What are the qualities of excellent facilitators?

One of the most useful outlines of facilitator qualities that we have come across is the list developed by Hislop (2000). It provides a useful outline of the characteristics of an excellent facilitator, it has been adapted here to include the skills of a facilitator working with virtual learning communities.

Motivated	Motivated facilitators have a strong interest in working to make their online community successful. They are willing to make the effort to deal with technology and create a working and learning environment.
Approachable	Approachable facilitators encourage members to interact with them. Being approachable reduces barriers to interaction in the online environment.
Visible	Visible facilitators make their presence felt frequently in the online environment. This helps add substance to the online experience and to provide glue to hold the community of learners together.

Explicit	Explicit facilitators provide timely, detailed directions about what the members need to do and how the community will operate. They are also explicit in addressing content. This helps to ameliorate the limitations of the restricted communication channels in the online environment.
Proactive	Proactive facilitators make an extra effort to reach out to members in ways beyond what would be necessary or typical in a traditional environment. For example, a proactive facilitator might put extra effort into contacting an inactive member in a learning community.
Discreet	Discreet facilitators manage a community without dominating it. They facilitate online discussions while encouraging members to provide most of the comments. They also know when to comment publicly and when to switch to private communication (telephone, e-mail) with a member or members.
Collaborative	Collaborative facilitators are willing to work with other people, for example sponsors, guest participants, as a means of supporting the community. They are also comfortable working with members in a coaching role rather than a more hierarchical style.
Technically capable	Technically capable facilitators have sufficient technical knowledge and adeptness to be comfortable with the online environment. Online facilitators do not need to be technical experts but they need basic technical skills to get started. They also need to be able to deal with the inevitable technical glitches and technology changes (with technical support help).
Credible	Members accept credible facilitators as experts in the subject of the learning community and also in their role in supporting the community.

This list may seem daunting to new facilitators and we do not want to deter our readers by promoting models of excellence that seem off-putting. It is offered here as a model of good practice.

New facilitators are likely to have some concerns about taking up their role and these may include some of the following:

- fears regarding technical skills;
- cynicism due to previous experience with virtual communications;
- concerns that the community will not work;

- time involved in learning new systems and processes;
- time involved in facilitating a new community;
- impersonal nature of online communications;
- workloads and other pressures.

It is important that these are addressed and one approach is to develop knowledge and expertise by taking part in online activities such as virtual conferences, online educational programmes or online meetings. Another approach is to develop experience through working with a co-facilitator.

Working with co-facilitators

Co-facilitating involves working with other colleagues and jointly facilitating the learning community. Co-facilitating offers a number of advantages:

- Different facilitators bring their own personalities, knowledge and skills, and experiences to the programme. Pairs, or trios, of facilitators working together can provide a much richer learning environment than any single individual.
- Different facilitators will have different virtual voices and this provides a variety of experiences for the learners. Again the presence of different voices with different approaches and perspectives provides a more stimulating learning environment than the voice of an individual facilitator.
- The workload can be shared, with individual facilitators taking responsibility for the development of resources, maintenance of the learning environment and introducing new activities.
- Individual facilitators can take responsibility for individual learners and/or small learning sets. This shares the workload and also enables the facilitator to focus in depth on particular learners, learning groups or activities.
- Facilitators can provide each other with support and feedback.
- Facilitators can provide each other with back-up, for example during holiday periods.

Probably the most important contributing factor to successful co-facilitating is the need for the co-facilitators to share the same or similar values and beliefs about professional development, learning and community participation. This will help to ensure that there are no irreconcilable differences during the life of the community. When starting to work as a co-facilitator it is worthwhile spending time discussing how the facilitation team will work together and also clarifying individual roles and responsibilities. It is important to build in time for facilitators to regularly discuss current issues and decide how they will be handled. This is important as it enables the facilitators to present a professional and coordinated presence in the learning community and it can also deter members from attempting to play one facilitator off against the other. The following quotation is from a facilitator:

I co-facilitated the learning community with Jonathan. We met for coffee each week to discuss our planned activities and interventions. This was of great value as we had really challenging times with the group, partly because they were so motivated and keen and partly because some of the members were difficult. At one stage one of the community refused to work. I really didn't know how to handle this situation but through brainstorming with Sam during coffee one morning we planned a strategy that was really successful. I felt much more confident about handling the situation because we were in agreement. Also, I think that we were more creative in the way that we managed ***** because we had been able to bounce ideas off each other.

Chris, facilitator

Levels of participation

All communities include individuals who participate in different ways and at different rates. Some members participate far more vociferously and far more frequently than others and this is sometimes a source of concern within the community, as illustrated in the following quotation:

I ran into Sue in the office earlier this week and she said that she had noticed that I've made a 'hell of a lot' of contributions to this community. I was certainly aware that I've been spending a lot of time online but I hadn't really thought about whether others had noticed how much I've been doing. What are other people's views on this? Do those of you who don't have as much time to spare feel 'freaked out' when you see how much work the more active members have contributed?

Barry

In this case the other participants offered reassurance:

Hi Barry

I'm certainly aware that you generate a large number of postings . . . I definitely sympathize with the freaked-out feeling when I compare the number of postings that I've made.

It should be remembered though that a lot of work goes on behind the scenes without a participant feeling the need to actually put finger to keyboard and post a message. This was my experience with the visiting expert, I read his paper, read all the postings about it but missed the deadline for submitting my own thoughts. Don't worry I'm going to post my thoughts after the deadline anyway!

I think that the number of postings made by any individual should not be related specifically to how much or how little work they have done.

Mandy

I think Mandy has made some interesting comments here and surely it links back to the learning styles we were thinking about earlier? Some people (like me) are quick to write thoughts down and tend to emphasize the spontaneous aspects (speaking before they think!), but others will be more reflective. The fact that some people don't post as many messages on to an electronic board must be similar to the idea that some colleagues will sit in a project planning meeting and not say anything and yet produce excellent work at the end of a project. For my part, although I have posted a few messages, it is sitting down and reflecting that I have trouble with. Lastly, I think that all virtual learning communities need people like Barry to keep them ticking over, because they die easily. If you look at other successful on-line communities, the same names appear over and over again – the Barrys of this world!

James

In virtual communities it is relatively easy for facilitators to track members who are active and contribute regularly and those whose level of participation could be a cause for concern. WebCT, for example, provides instructor tracking tools that provide instant information on the total number of postings individual participants have read and posted. In other ICT platforms facilitators need to work a little harder to track participation levels but facilitators soon develop skills in spotting participants whose participation levels are low.

During the induction phase facilitators need to ensure that all members have joined the virtual learning community and sent at least one message. We have found that if someone doesn't appear online in the first few days of the life of the community then it is useful to phone them and find out if they are having problems accessing the site etc. Sometimes there are simple technical issues that can be quickly resolved over the phone. In some cases we have found that members haven't understood the initial documentation or briefing and so missed the start date.

The facilitator needs to monitor interaction levels throughout the community life cycle and it is particularly important to identify levels of very high participation (is the member dominating the community?) and also levels of low or non-existent participation (are quieter members dropping out or are they just observing what is happening within the community and learning by 'lurking'? see p. 126). Some ICT infrastructures provide summaries of the number of times each participant enters the virtual environment and some provide a more detailed analysis and will identify how many postings each participant has read. This can be useful in helping facilitators to make informed judgements about individual participant needs.

We have found it helpful to be explicit with participants when they express concern about their low levels of contribution or even when they compare their knowledge skills and understanding with others in the group. This is illustrated in the following quotations from a discussion group where Alison posted this response to a facilitator's question asking participants to reflect on their experience during the incubation phase of a virtual community.

I would like to say that it has been a new and exciting experience throughout – but I'd be lying. The reptilian part of my brain kicked in for the first two tasks and for most of the learning experience so far. The summary for Activity 2 listed the following as causes of learner stress:

> Stress in an e-learning situation may be caused by one or more factors and some people are more resilient to stress than others. The following factors frequently cause stress and are likely to have an impact on learning:
>
> • fear of technology (that's me!);
> • fear of entering a new learning environment (that's me!);
> • disorientation within a virtual environment (that's definitely me!);
> • lack of confidence about finding their voice in a virtual environment (me!);
> • poor sight or hearing (having just had to buy glasses for the first time in a long time that's me!) etc.

Up until last night (3 January), I felt some of the above. I was extremely worried and confused about what I am doing, how I'm doing it. I am better at learning facts and theories and this online community has, right from the beginning, asked us to put forward our opinions and take on board new experiences and grasp concepts that are new to me and I feel very intimidated by the online environment itself.

So, given the above you would think my experiences to date have all been very negative but they haven't. Admittedly, the last few weeks with all the computer problems have set me back a bit, but slowly, bit by bit, I'm feeling more comfortable with the environment. Everyone has been encouraging and knowing that I don't come from an academic background and am definitely the most 'IT challenged' in the group, people have gone out of their way to help and encourage me. The group work has been interesting, I only appeared in one chat room conversation and there were only three of us and I found that I had hesitant fingers and brain coordination – by the time I'd typed a sentence the conversation had moved on and, despite reading the netiquette, I couldn't remember any of it in the live chat room (I'd be no good on *Who Wants to be a Millionaire!*).

I had a verbal breakdown today (8th) by Terry as to What my group has done since my machine died and I feel that I'd never be as inventive on my own, though I do feel a complete slacker as I haven't been able to contribute much – due to 'technology' or in my case lack of it. Though I have yet to find my voice, I feel that I am slowly finding my feet and haven't been abandoned by the wayside by my group but more carried along with them.

Alison

The facilitator offered reassurance as follows:

> Thanks Alison for your direct honesty, your reflections on your experience during the group activity remind me of Etienne Wenger's work. He has written extensively on 'Communities of Practice' and talks of insider and outsider status within communities. He talks of the outsider status of new or inexperienced members of communities and identifies the importance of 'legitimate peripheral participation'.
>
> He suggests that through legitimate peripheral participation outsiders learn know-how, develop experience and grow in confidence and move towards insider status within the community. It sounds as if you are occupying a position of legitimate peripheral participation and our community is offering you the right amount of support as you feel that you are not being abandoned but being carried along.
>
> If you're interested, there is a growing literature on his work a couple of URLs are:
>
> http://www.parc.xerox.com/ops/members/brown/papers/
> orglearning.html
>
> and
>
> http://www.co-i-1.com/coil/knowledge-garden/cop/1ss.shtml
>
> It will be interesting to monitor your progress as this community develops, for the time being enjoy your legitimate peripheral participation. I note that most of us seem to have spent time outside our comfort zones during this experience. Emphasizing the need for a supportive community.
>
> Yours reflecting further on how the community can be used to grow confidence and extend comfort zones,
>
> Dina

During the next face-to-face session another participant commented on how valuable and reassuring she had found this particular posting. An analysis of contributions to that community show that Alison's participation levels increased as the life cycle developed. Early nurturing was significant. Facilitators need to create an environment where participants feel accepted, and if this is achieved it can lead the group to exciting changes and developments.

There is a growing literature on the subject of 'lurkers' or 'browsers'. Lurkers or browsers are virtual community members who do not comment or actively engage in activities or discussions online very often, if at all. Gilly Salmon (2000) quotes research in the Open University that indicates that within any given online group it is likely that 30 per cent will actively participate, 30 per cent will lurk/browse and 30 per cent will drop out. This same research also emphasizes that although lurkers and browsers are not actively participating most are, in fact, actively learning from the discussions and activities of the community. Our experience has been more positive than the Open University figures would suggest and our lurker/browser rate has never been as high as 30 per cent throughout a whole community life cycle.

End of community evaluations and focus group discussions have also revealed the high levels of learning taking place by participants who are observing the community and learning from the side. It is also important to note that participation levels also fluctuate for a variety of work-related reasons. When we were working with the steel workers there were definite dates within their working calendar when we could predict participation levels would drop, shut-downs within the rolling mills for maintenance were notoriously low participation times and we adapted community activities to allow for this.

Wenger (1998) introduced the concept of legitimate peripheral participation to describe the behaviours of some group members in communities of practice. He also noted that low participation levels do not equate with low learning levels and he argued that some community members are engaged in dynamic learning processes just through being exposed to the learning of others even though they seem to be contributing very little. He argued that all communities have significant numbers of members who occupy positions of legitimate peripheral participation. He says that in effective communities members accept that participants engage in the community in different ways, for example people with less experience learn through association and social interactions with colleagues with more experience. He extends this idea to compare the way in which those on the periphery of a community of practice learn with the way in which apprentices traditionally learnt through being apprenticed to master practitioners. Apprentices started off their professional training by being accepted as valued members of a professional community even though their initial contribution to the profession was minimal, their position as low contributors was accepted, respected and understood. They were learning through association, through observing and listening to the narratives and practices of experienced practitioners.

Wenger's work demonstrates the importance of creating spaces within our communities for low participation levels to be acceptable. In any community individual participation levels fluctuate and it is important to recognize that this is a natural part of the life of a community.

Individuals who are normally high participators may move onto the periphery as a result of other pressures in their work/lives, members who lack confidence at the beginning of the community may suddenly find their online voice and find that their online contributions are becoming more and more frequent. Individuals may find that they are particularly interested or particularly expert in one aspect of community activity or discussion, they may find that their contributions are essential and core to the community field of knowledge for a time.

Patterns of participation raise different issues for facilitators of learning communities. Experienced facilitators develop a respect for the natural ebb and flow of community participation levels and develop skill in recognizing when low participation levels indicate lack of satisfaction with the community and when low participation levels are due to other pressures. In communities where there is a changing membership then there is a need to support the departure of members and the arrival of new members. This can be quite a challenge as new members need to be brought up-to-date with community activities so that they can become active members, that is to move from legitimate peripheral participation to full participation as effectively as possible. Box 7.4 provides a set of questions that facilitators (and also participants) may find useful to ask themselves throughout the life of the community.

Box 7.4   Questions for facilitators

- What are the levels of activity and participation?
- Is anyone not participating?
- What are the reasons for low participation levels?
- Are the participants supporting each other?
- Has everyone's message obtained at least one response?
- Can collaborative support be further encouraged?
- What are the current issues in the community?
- Are you accessing the site regularly enough?

Summary

This chapter has explored how members and facilitators can contribute to the healthy life of a community. Members need to develop their skills so that they can manage their time, read and follow a large number of threads and deal with potential information overload, develop an online voice, actively participate in community learning activities, and also learn to flexibly adopt different roles and responsibilities. The attributes of an effective facilitator are discussed and a useful approach to developing these skills involves working with co-facilitators. The chapter concluded with an examination of member and facilitator participation levels.

8

Social Learning in Virtual Learning Communities

Introduction

The aim of this chapter is to explore the learning processes that take place within learning communities and to identify opportunities for enhancing and sustaining effective learning. We have deliberated long and hard over the content of this chapter as learning and the transformative power of learning to change the lives and professional identity of community practitioners is the central focus of our work. However, concepts of learning are complex and messy and we have not found one coherent model or theory of learning that captures our experience of learning in and with and through communities in all its rich complexity. Our understanding is constantly unravelling and reconfiguring to accommodate new aspects of experience or theoretical research that we had not previously considered.

We approach this chapter from the perspective of facilitators with a commitment to constructivism; we do not try to provide answers or endorse clear-cut theoretical frameworks. Rather we attempt to share with the reader some of the complementary, conflicting and inconsistent theories and concepts that have helped us to work towards an understanding of the processes involved in supporting and participating effectively in community learning. We seek to encourage the reader to consider some of the major influences on our work, however, we have been influenced by the work of so many different theorists, researchers, colleagues and community participants that it would be impossible to mention them all here: instead we hope that the range of ideas covered will be viewed as a starting point.

We challenge you as our readers to build your own individual understanding and develop your own list of seminal thinkers, favourite articles, books and personal theories that fit with your own real experiences of facilitating and learning in communities. We make no apologies for the fact that our examples and selections might be seen as idiosyncratic, we do not pretend to present one all-embracing, neatly integrated theory of community learning; rather we offer some of the complex and even paradoxical ideas and concepts that have made a real and positive impact on our understanding and practice.

Socially orientated theories of learning

A good starting point is to consider socially oriented theories of learning. In a nut shell, these emphasize the importance of human interactions within the process of learning. Broadly speaking our seminal theorists Lave and Wenger, Wang and Bonk, Vygotsky, Laurillard and the others mentioned in this chapter agree that individuals learn as a result of interactions with others within a particular social context, for example work, a programme of study, a learning community. They also agree that what we learn depends on who we are, what we want to become and what we value. Socially oriented theories of learning are particularly relevant to us if we are interested in supporting group or community learning.

Perhaps a good starting point is to consider Goodyear's summary (2000) of underpinning principles of socially orientated learning adapted from Darrouzet and Lynn (1999):

- learning is fundamentally social;
- learning is integrated into the life of communities;
- learning is an act of participation;
- knowing depends on engagement in practice;
- engagement is inseparable from empowerment;
- failure to learn is the result of exclusion from participation;
- people are natural lifelong learners.

We have found it useful to think of socially oriented theories of learning as falling into three main perspectives: **constructivism**, **Soviet socio-cultural theory**, and **situated cognition**. As you will see, these three ways of thinking about learning are not mutually exclusive and there is some conflict and some overlap between them. Where possible we offer practical examples of how these three perspectives and theoretical frameworks for thinking about learning could be applied to the groups in which we have worked.

Constructivism

Every theorist, academic and participant seems to have a different and personalized understanding of the concept of **constructivism** and this can make it difficult to grasp at first. It is a slippery concept and difficult to capture within one statement, some helpful definitions include:

> Constructivists view learning as the result of mental construction. Students learn by fitting new information together with what they already know. People learn best when they actively construct their own understanding.
>
> (Van Ryneveld, no date)

> From a constructivist perspective, learning is an active process in which learners construct new ideas or concepts based on their current and past knowledge. In order to help [learners] do this [facilitators] engage

in a process of 'scaffolding' in which they encourage [learners] to discover principles themselves, rather than by telling them.

(A. Lillejohn and C. Higgison, LTSN Generic Centre e-Learning Series,
A guide for teachers)

Knowledge is discovered by learners and transformed into concepts learners can relate to. It is then reconstructed and expanded through new learning experiences. Learning consists of active participation by the learner versus passive acceptance of information presented by an expert lecturer. Learning comes about through transactions and dialogue among learners and between faculty and learners, in a social setting. Learners learn to understand and appreciate different perspectives through a dialogue with their peers.

(Panitz 1996: 1)

Knowledge construction occurs when participants explore issues, take positions, discuss their positions in an argumentative format and reflect on and re-evaluate their positions.

(Jonassen 1995: 16)

Our understanding of the learning processes within successful communities owes much to the ideas behind the concept of knowledge construction. The 'constructivists', for example Jonassen, Panitz and Dillenbourg to name a few, view knowledge as something which is actively constructed by learners through discussion and negotiation with others, for example: with their colleagues, peers, facilitators, fellow practitioners and experts in their field, this process of engagement with others results in the construction of common understandings and shared meanings. Learning communities provide an ideal environment for community members to exchange and interrogate their world maps or mental models; clarify the meaning of a topic or professional practice and deconstruct and reconstruct its constituent parts; identify and explore links between theory and practice; and also share their work and academic or professional experiences with each other. For example:

Being part of a learning community helped me to see things in a new way, I found that I was extending my understanding of how things work in the Trust. The fact that I was listened to and encouraged to contribute left me thinking that some of my ideas were right, I felt confident to suggest changes to our practices that might work.

Anne, Primary Care Trust

At first I just read what the others had to say I didn't want to appear foolish, but I soon realized that in some areas I knew more than most of the others. Once I started joining in I found that I was gaining confidence and making suggestions that even surprised myself. I found that I was considering other people's points of view and changing the way that I thought about things, somehow its made me more open to new suggestions.

Terence, IT trainer

As a group we produced so much more than any of us could have achieved on our own – what we produced seemed to be more than the sum of our parts. It was such a good feeling.

Debbie, Administrator

The following characteristics are associated with constructivism:

- learning viewed as a process and 'how' individuals learn is important;
- there is an emphasis on sharing knowledge and understanding;
- power relationships are less hierachical – those with less experience and knowledge and understanding work with those with more;
- all learners' opinions valued and respected;
- collective commitment to mutual support;
- individual life and work experience is valued and affirmed;
- learners build on previous knowledge and understanding;
- learners engage in dialogues and discourse, critical inquiry is valued;
- critical reflection is fundamental to the experience;
- the learning process empowers individuals and identities are transformed.

The concept of knowledge construction is often linked to collaborative groupwork and collaborative learning. It is worth noting here that many people seem to use the terms collaborative and cooperative interchangeably and this can lead to confusion. Rochelle and Teasley (1995) offer a useful distinction: they say that cooperative work 'is accomplished by the division of labour among participants, as an activity where each person is responsible for a portion of the problem solving' . . . whereas collaboration involves . . . 'the mutual engagement of participants in a co-ordinated effort to solve the problem together'. The following working definitions reflect our understanding of the distinctions between cooperative and collaborative learning:

Cooperative working includes sharing resources, exchanging information and giving and receiving feedback. Typically, cooperative working involves individuals working towards individual goals and outcomes and benefiting from working in a supportive group. If there is an end product it is often possible to identify who contributed to different parts of it.

Collaborative learning groups are likely to involve e-learners working together on a shared goal. This may be a goal that they have agreed and negotiated themselves, or it may be a goal set up by a facilitator or fellow learner. Examples include learners working on a joint project, practitioners working together on a joint report or academic article, or colleagues working together on a joint work-based project. If there is an end product it is extremely difficult to differentiate different participant's contributions.

Cooperative working
An example of cooperative working is shown in Box 8.1.

Box 8.1   Example of planned cooperative working within a learning community

---

A public sector organization identified a staff training and development need in the area of project management and an urgent need to equip eight relatively new staff with the skills they required to undertake immediate projects. After some consultation a strategy was developed that would enable these staff to attend a number of half-day workshops on project management skills and then to work on their projects with the help and support of their trainer and also each other. During the first face-to-face workshop the eight participants were introduced to the idea of an online learning community and given access to a virtual learning environment. At the end of this workshop the participants agreed an action plan with the external trainer and this included working on their live projects and presenting their work, for example project specification, project plan, to the learning community for feedback.

For the next three months participants worked on their projects and at each stage in the project management cycle they presented their work for feedback from the other members of the learning community. Participation in the virtual community followed a distinct cycle of patterns of high activity, when members shared their work and gave each other feedback, followed by periods of low activity when members were focused on working on their individual projects in their workplace. The community used the discussion forum as a means of sharing ideas, good practice and feedback on their project work. The final evaluation of the learning community showed that members found it a valuable means of support and feedback while they were putting their new project management skills into practice. Feedback was particularly valuable in giving a different perspective on the project.

Quotes from participants on the Project Management Training Programme

> I got a lot out of working in this way, I found the feedback sessions very helpful, it was good to bounce ideas off the others then go back to my project and implement changes. I felt sharper and more motivated.
>
> Chris

> It suited the way I work, I like to get on with my own thing, but its good to have a sounding board every now and then. I think my project management skills are much better now, I learnt a lot just from reading about how the others were implementing things, time management was a big thing for me.
>
> Alison

Collaborative working

Knowledge construction is often the outcome of collaborative working. The term collaborative is also challenging to define and Dillenbourg (1999) offers a broad definition that suggests that collaborative learning is 'a situation in which two or more people attempt to learn something together' and he deconstructs this statement in the following way:

- **'two or more'** – a pair, small group (3–5), class (20–30), a community (100s or 1000s of people), a society (10,000s or 1,000,000);
- **'learn something'** – 'follow a course', 'study course material', 'perform learning activities such as problem solving', 'learn from lifelong work practice', etc;
- **'together'** may involve different forms of interaction: face-to-face; computer-mediated – synchronous or asynchronous, frequent in time or not, a truly joint effort or involving the division of labour.

We have found that collaborative approaches to learning result in individual learners having a deeper understanding of the subject/information/profession/practice and the participants seem to engage in higher quality thinking strategies. Our findings are supported by other researchers, for example McConnell (2000) concludes that achievement is generally higher in collaborative situations rather than individualistic or competitive ones.

The example in Box 8.2 demonstrates how collaborative activities can have many benefits.

Box 8.2   Example of collaborative working within a learning community

We have previously mentioned the learning community that we facilitated at Birmingham University. This was a community developed through a series of face-to-face and online workshops and activities and provided the first opportunity for academics, IT trainers and information services staff to participate together in a continuing professional development programme. Staff development programmes at the University of Birmingham had previously been delivered to either academic or support service staff separately. The innovative nature of this integrated team approach led to many examples of collaborative learning.

This learning community involved staff working together on a series of collaborative activities, for example one very successful activity involved preparing a presentation for a university department of their choice on the value of working in integrated professional teams to develop blended learning programmes and resources. The quality of the final presentations illustrated the benefits of collaborative working, that is they were produced to a high technical specification, with rich examples of web-based resources directly targeted at the subject specialisms of the chosen department. The content was presented in such a way as to appeal to all members of staff interested in providing the best possible quality learning experience for their students. The finished products were seamless, that is, it was impossible to identify the person who had contributed to each part of the final presentation. In addition to being used to brief departments on the benefits of working in integrated curriculum development teams the presentations were also used in a number of different ways, for example to inform staff across the university of the potential for integrated team working at the Learning Development Unit open days and also as the basis for conference papers. One participant from the learning community also had a paper published on the theme of integrated professional teams.

Other benefits of this experience of working collaboratively to construct new knowledge and understanding were that different participants from within the community also began to collaborate together outside the guided community activities in their professional roles in the University. The participants had internalized the value of working collaboratively across different professional groups and departments, and transferred this practice outside the learning community.

Quotes from participants on collaborative learning

The small group presentation activity really took me out of my comfort zone but it was a great learning experience. It seemed such a short amount of time to complete it in and it had to be done in collaboration with people I didn't know and couldn't even remember what they looked like! This was a totally new experience for me but I was with a great group and I think we carried it off successfully (thanks to Jane Brown's hard work!) I did enjoy the challenge that the experience posed and we achieved so much more than I could have done on my own.

I'm amazed by how well and how quickly the groups worked together. Our collaboration took place completely online and we were all really pleased with the results.

I've never worked in this way before, I don't think it would have worked if we hadn't established trust between us. Some of the others put more into the preparation than me but there wasn't any resentment, we all did what we could, work pressures permitting. It was great to feel that was OK. Next time I'll try to do more than my fair share it should work out fair in the end. You can achieve so much more when you are working with colleagues who are supportive not competitive.

Some of the many benefits of cooperative and collaborative learning that we have experienced include:

- better working relationships;
- increased motivation;
- improved problem solving;
- sparking off ideas, generating more ideas, sharing ideas;
- generally encouraging a more supportive work culture;
- innovation in the development of work-related products;
- new work practices;
- service improvements;
- improved confidence in individuals' professional identity and capability leading to a more proactive approach to work and practice;
- out of the box thinking;
- improved team working;
- more strategic thinking.

Does collaborative learning work for everyone? Some people, for example Jensen (1996) and Garratt (1997), suggest that learners will have different preferences for working together independently, cooperatively or collabora- tively and that this is likely to reflect individual learning style. This suggests that some learners may be less successful in learning communities or programmes built around collaborative or cooperative work (Box 8.3).

Box 8.3   Example of an unhappy group member

Barbara Allan was a member of a virtual learning community that comprised 12 members representing different professional back- grounds (lecturing, librarianship, IT and management). The com- munity was developed in response to an organizational issue that needed a cross-department group to tackle it. Individual community members volunteered to join the community and experiment with the possibilities that virtual learning communities appeared to offer. The community appeared to get off to a good start. However, one member, 'Suzanne', appeared to be unhappy with working in the community. After some discussions it transpired that when she volunteered for the project she thought working in a virtual community wouldn't involve her in working with others (which she hated). She left the community and was quite adamant that the e-mails asking for volunteers should have stressed the need for working in online groups in the virtual community.

Soviet socio-cultural theory

Vygotsky's (1978) work has also influenced us. He suggested that learners are capable of performing at higher intellectual levels when they are asked to work in group situations rather than when they work individually. Vygotsky talked about the 'zone of proximal development' and suggested that learners learn more effectively when they are guided by an 'expert'. Talking with and interrogating the 'expert' allows learners to refine their thinking and ideas. This enables the learner to build or construct new concepts from their existing knowledge and thus the zone of peripheral development links directly with current 'constructivist theories of adult learning'. This idea also links directly with the concept of cognitive apprenticeship, that is learning from someone who is more skilled within the broader heading of socio-cultural theories of learning. The concept of cognitive apprenticeship (Wang and Bonk 2001) is based on traditional apprenticeship and it explores learning from the viewpoint of a new practitioner developing knowledge and skills by observing and learning from expert practice. Cognitive apprenticeship may involve face-to-face and/or virtual communication processes, it is embedded within authentic work practices and involves a range of different instructional methods as well as social activities.

Collins *et al.* (1989) provide a useful framework of six instructional methods of cognitive apprenticeship:

1. Modelling, where the new practitioner learns from observing and copying an expert's practices. Barbara Allan experienced this type of learning when she was a member of the MEd programme which involved participating in a virtual community for two years. One of the tutors offered a role model of excellence in establishing rapport with learners and managing the interpersonal aspects of community participation. Barbara used his practice as the basis for her own online facilitation activities.
2. Coaching, where the new practitioner is supported through one-to-one support that is likely to include goal setting, instruction, practice, feedback. Examples of this approach took place in an e-mentoring project where aspiring women managers were provided with online coaching by experienced practitioners (Headlam-Wells 2004). This project is outlined in Box 8.4.
3. Scaffolding, where the experienced practitioner provides temporary support to the learner for those parts of the task that they find difficult. This support may initially be extremely active and then the experienced practitioner may fade out as they gradually remove their support in response to the new practitioner developing their competence and confidence. Scaffolding could be seen in the experiences of the Birmingham e-learning community where members with particular expertise provided support and structure for their colleagues, for example in the use of ICT, and the development of new practices in relationship to learning and teaching.

Box 8.4   Empathy project

The European-funded EMPATHY project (E-Mentoring for Profes-sionals at Hull University) adopted a solution-based approach to the problem of women's under-representation at senior management levels. Research showed that most successful women managers had benefited from having a mentor. The project started from the belief that a particular learning community that offered mentoring as its *raison d'être* would have beneficial career outcomes. The EMPATHY project enabled 28 mentoring pairs to work together through a blended mixture of face-to-face and online contacts. The online con-tacts enabled the women to overcome barriers of time, geography and organizational boundaries. For many women it helped overcome feelings of professional isolation. The project was successful as indicated by the evaluation process, for example some women obtain-ing career progression, the continuation of some mentoring pairs (Headlam-Wells 2004).

---

4. Articulation, where the new practitioner discusses their issue or problem and explores it with the guidance of the more experienced practitioner. A specific example of this could be found in the project management community where a few community members were frustrated and chal-lenged by the differences between the theory and practice of project management. Online discussions helped them to articulate these issues and also it helped them to gain confidence in the importance of their practical experience and the need to manage their projects in a style that would work for them in their organization even if this meant that it didn't match textbook 'best practice'.
5. Reflection enables the new practitioner to externalize their internal thinking processes, and discussion with more experienced practitioners facilitates this process further. This is likely to involve a process that includes evaluation, exploring other options or ways of behaving, and action planning. We have built in the process of reflection in all of our virtual learning communities.
6. Exploration, where the new practitioner is involved in work-based prob-lem solving. The more experienced practitioner may set guidelines, make suggestions for action, and enable the learner to understand and appreciate the complexity of the problem, underlying issues and its con-text. An example of this approach was used in the project management virtual community and also with the steel workers.

As the examples illustrate, virtual communication tools are being used increasingly to support cognitive apprenticeship, tools such as e-mail, virtual discussion groups and chat rooms provide a medium through which new entrants to a profession can learn from more experienced practitioners without the need for face-to-face meetings. This process is often managed through formal mentoring schemes. In the context of professional training programmes the concept of cognitive apprenticeship provides a framework for the development of work-based learning activities, for example through the use of case studies or problem-solving activities in both face-to-face and e-learning situations. Finally, the process of cognitive apprenticeship may also lead individual practitioners to become members of communities of practice as their mentor or expert guide supports them in becoming part of an established professional community.

Situated cognition

The concept of situated cognition relates to the entry of learners into a community and offers a way of understanding how community participants learn to learn and work within this community. The community may be located within an educational institution or, as Lave and Wenger (1991) suggest, it may take place outside educational contexts, for example within professions or commercial organizations with employees with high levels of technical expertise. They suggest that these learning communities must be in existence over a period of time as Wenger states:

> The development of practice takes time, but what defines a community of practice in its temporal dimension is not just a specific minimum of time . . . [but] . . . Sustaining enough mutual engagement in pursuing an enterprise together to share some significant learning . . . communities of practice can be thought of as shared histories of learning.
> (Wenger 1998: 86)

The work of Lave and Wenger (1991) is based on a number of assumptions about learning, learners, knowledge, and knowing and meaning.

1. **Learners are social beings** and interactions with others are a core component of learning activities and situations.
2. **Knowledge** is a matter of competence with respect to valued enterprises.
3. **Knowing** is a matter of participating in the pursuit of such enterprises, that is, of active engagement in the world.
4. **Meaning** is our ability to make connections between ideas and individual experience and is ultimately what learning is to produce.

Wenger identifies four types of discourse that involve community participants in activities that will support community growth. When facilitating communities or designing learning activities that will encourage knowledge construction within our communities, we should encourage discourses that engage the participants in focusing on the following:

1. **Meaning**: a way of talking about our (changing) ability – individually and collectively – to experience our life and the world as meaningful.

2. **Practice**: a way of talking about shared historical and social resources, frameworks, and perspectives that can sustain mutual engagement in action.
3. **Community**: a way of talking about the social configurations in which our enterprises are defined as worth pursuing and our participation is recognizable as competence.
4. **Identity**: a way of talking about how learning changes who we are and creates personal histories of becoming master practitioners in the context of our communities.

Effective learning communities involve members in a process of mutual engagement, shared or joint enterprise, and the types of activities that support this are outlined in Table 8.1.

Lave and Wenger (1991) also introduced the concept of 'legitimate peripheral participation', that is the process by which newcomers to the community move from a position of minimal peripheral participation or outsider status to one of full community membership and insider status. The importance of accepting that community members participate at different levels depending on their levels of experience and expertise is explored in more depth in Chapter 7.

Transformational learning

> Moving toward full participation in practice involves not just a greater commitment of time, intensified effort, more and broader responsibilities within the community, and more difficult and risky tasks, but more significantly, an increasing sense of identity as a master practitioner.
>
> (Lave and Wenger 1991)

Table 8.1 Activities to stimulate engagement and enterprise

Concept	Activities
Mutual engagement	Members select their topic, problem or issue
	Members work on a real-life issue or problem
	Members negotiate responsibilities within the group
	Members set their own boundaries and deadlines
	Online activities require individuals to share their knowledge, skills and experience
Joint enterprise	Facilitator to assume the role of mentor
	Activities that enable members to negotiate goals and working processes
	Reflective activities during the process
	Encourage development of multiple viewpoints
	Allow for individuals to take on different roles at different times
Shared enterprise	Members share work and work towards same goal
	Members exchange information and ideas
	Include virtual visitors

So far this chapter has considered key concepts that have helped to shape our understanding and experience of constructivist approaches to collaborative learning. However, what we are really interested in, is working with learning communities to transform the identities of the community participants, that is increasing each community participant's sense of identity as a competent professional or master practitioner. The test of our effectiveness as facilitators is the impact that the learning experiences have had on the identities of those involved in the learning community. Box 8.5 illustrates the transformational learning that may take place over a period of time within a learning community.

Box 8.5   Example of transformational learning

Jim was a recently promoted middle manager in an industrial cleaning company servicing the steel works in a northern city in the UK. He had had no previous managerial experience but had proved himself to be hard working, committed and loyal to the company, able to use his initiative and well respected by peers and colleagues. He had little confidence in his ability as a manager and his line manager suggested that he should undertake training in management skills as a priority. Jim was invited to join a small group of middle managers who were involved in a pilot transferable management skills training programme in the region.

We were involved in this initiative and established a virtual learning community to support this training. Jim participated in the learning community for over 18 months and achieved a 60 credit university award in management skills. Formative and summative evaluations tracked Jim's growing confidence and his transformation in professional identity He started out lacking in confidence and not even sure how to handle basic managerial functions, as the following postings in the learning community discussion forum demonstrate.

Month 1, May 2002
Evening all
Not sure I'm up to this university training, I'm a shi* shoveler at heart but I'm going to have a go at it. It's a great day for a barby anyone for a beer?
Jim

Month 5, September 2002
Good morning from Sunny Scunny
Just a quick note to say that I also enjoyed last Wednesday's session. I had to give two tool box talks last Friday and the work that we did last Weds helped me to deliver them more professionally.

My talk was planned in detail, I handed out an agenda, listing what was to be discussed, including minutes of the last meeting. I stuck to the time schedule and kept it to 30 minutes and we covered safety topics, accidents, how the company is doing in general, how the area contract is progressing. I think I came across in a professional manner by being more confident and answering all questions without hesitation. I was even popping in the odd funny just like in the face-to-face sessions.
Jim

The following posting was sent towards the end of the formal learning community training programme. The participants had been asked to prepare a presentation on continuous improvement practices at work. Jim decided that he would present his presentation to his senior management team.

Month 17, September 2003
Hello everyone,
I'll make the following points during my presentation to the senior managers:

1.   All supervisors and operators should fill in vehicle defect reports and attend a seminar on how to make active use of the vehicle defect reporting system. Obviously this would have to be developed but it wouldn't take much effort!
2.   We should contact plant manufacturers to provide training courses for our engineers. This will hopefully give them at the very least a refresher of information that they may already know.
3.   Maintenance engineers to arrange for suppliers to deliver the spare parts rather than the engineers leaving site for an hour or two.
4.   Pre-planning preventative maintenance – How many times do our maintenance engineers contact us for servicing or preventative maintenance? Clearly more communication between departments is needed.
5.   I believe that sharing knowledge is a problem between the engineers. It is a fact that different engineers have different specialist knowledge in different subjects, e.g. AUT electrical or hydraulics. If these people shared their experiences and knowledge we would have a more flexible and efficient team, thus not reliant on any particular person for a particular job or even avoiding the need to call in a contractor.

If any of you have any further comments or suggestions on this please let me know before next week, September 24th at latest.
Thanks
Jim

The transformation in Jim's identity is clear. He experienced a transformation that changed his perception of himself as someone who at heart was a hard-working operative to his perception of himself as a manager with the ability to identify continuous improvement practices and the ability to address his senior management team with confidence. Recently we invited Jim to contribute to a national conference on Lifelong Learning. He gave a presentation to an audience of over 150 health professionals and talked about the transforming power of learning communities such as the one that he had participated in.

The process of transformational learning that we have observed taking place in so many of the learning communities in which we have worked seems to be linked to the process of acculturation. When individual identities are changed the individuals involved seem to assimilate the customs, values, beliefs and practices of another culture or group of professionals or practitioners and this provides a way of understanding the process of transformation. A process of acculturation takes place in successful learning communities, as shown in Box 8.6.

Box 8.6   Example: Amanda's experience of acculturation within a learning community

Between 2000 and 2002 Amanda took part in an online learning community that was set up within the framework of a Master's programme in e-learning. Amanda had never experienced an e-learning community before. Unfortunately, she started the programme late and when she first logged into the environment it was clear that other members had already been conversing with each other in a Blackboard-based discussion group for several weeks. As a 'late' arrival Amanda initially felt isolated and on the edge of the community. Observing the online messages she felt as if everyone knew each other and lots of jokes appeared to be flying around the virtual environment. However, community members and tutors welcomed Amanda through friendly messages, acknowledging her messages and involving her in the community activities. Over the next few months Amanda became comfortable about working in the learning community and gradually developed her own style and approach to online communities, and found her virtual voice. In addition, she developed the customs and practices of the community facilitators (online tutors) and her peers. At the start of this experience Amanda always described herself as a novice e-learner and would use phrases such as 'I'm still wearing my L-plates' to illustrate that she was very much a learner. By the end of the programme Amanda clearly recognized herself as an experienced e-learner, community member and facilitator and said 'As a result of this group I am now ready to set up my own learning community in the college. There is a group of us who need to learn more about the practice of e-learning and I'm now willing and able to set up and steer the new college e-learning group. One of the best things about being a member of the learning community is that a number of us are going to continue it so I feel as if I'll have continuous help and support and be able to help and support others too.'

Summary

This chapter has focused on the importance of social interactions in the learning process. Individuals may move from a position of peripheral participation to one of full engagement with the learning community. As a result of this process they experience the process of acculturation and develop the customs, practices, values and beliefs of the learning community and, in doing so, become experienced or master practitioners. Community facilitators may support this process by enabling community members to engage in collaborative or cooperative learning activities and these have been explored through a series of examples including case studies, project work and individual examples. The learning processes that take place within learning communities are not linear or cyclical, and dynamic learning communities definitely shift participants towards higher levels of professional confidence, practice, expertise or knowledge and understanding. Table 8.2 below allows for individual progression without suggesting that this progression is straightforwardly incremental.

Table 8.2 Individual experiences in a learning community

Individual experience	Collaborative community learning experience supporting acculturation process	The transformation
Individual learning activity	Collaborative activities Narratives Conversations challenging perspectives, values and beliefs Shared understanding	New professional identity as experienced or master practitioner
World picture remains unchallenged	Readjustment of world picture	New world picture
Unassimilated information	Knowledge construction Collaboration	Knowledge management Authority
Lack of mastery	Acculturation	Mastery of practice
Lack of professional confidence	Conversation	Confidence promotion

9

Time and Participation in Learning Communities

Shortage of time to access and engage with online learning communities is a frequent issue for community members and facilitators. The purpose of this chapter is to explore virtual time issues and to provide a range of practical strategies to help community members and facilitators overcome the time demands of taking part in a community.

Very early in our work with learning communities we noticed that, for many people, time is a key issue and one of the most important factors in determining whether or not individual participants become active and effective community members. Time is such a significant issue for many community members that we decided to dedicate a whole chapter to exploring time-related issues in detail. We found that members regularly commented on their desire to become more actively engaged in the community and cited time constraints as being the single greatest barrier to effective participation. Individual members commented on their struggles in managing large workloads, their need to manage crises, problems and new initiatives at work, and their desire to maintain a reasonably healthy life/work balance. At the same time we observed that for many participants one of the most significant adjustments that they made in becoming actively engaged in an online community involved reflecting on and developing new time management strategies. As a result of this observation we began researching members' perceptions of time in face-to-face sessions and also through the online discussion groups, questionnaires and interviews. The outcomes of this research are summarized and presented in this chapter.

Different ways of perceiving time

Time is a human construct that can be explored in a number of different ways, through reviewing the literature on time we identified two useful ways of viewing it: clock or calendar time (sometimes called 'through-time') and experiential time (sometimes called 'in-time' or 'in the now'). Clock and calendar time is used to structure daily life and work in a myriad of ways in the modern world. In this approach time is perceived as a timeline with events happening at timed intervals. Individuals may observe their own timeline using tools such as diaries, milestones, calendars and deadlines.

Another approach to thinking about time is to fully experience or live in the present or 'now'. In this experiential approach to time individuals will 'go with the flow' and carry out activities when 'it feels right' or when they are mentally prepared for the event. Typically, individuals operating under this approach to time are living in the present and they don't prioritize the use of diaries, calendars, etc. In reality the approach an individual takes to managing and utilizing time will depend on their own personal relationship with time and their context. Individual preferences may be for living and working 'through-time' or 'in-time' and this may vary according to context. For example:

- A member of a learning community who is working on a high-profile organizational problem starts each day by entering the community site and responding to overnight messages, for example from colleagues working in different time zones. He then keeps this site minimized on his computer and accesses it as and when he has 'spare' time. On average he spends an hour each day working in the community.
- A colleague who is involved in a collaborative project based around a virtual learning community that is developing a set of learning resources has scheduled her access into the community site twice a week for an hour each time. She occasionally visits the site at additional times too.

Time and virtual communications

Our research has highlighted that many people who work together or learn together using virtual communications tools appear to require a different approach to time management than for traditional ways of communicating and working. The tools provided in community software enable individuals to access their community either in real time (using synchronous tools such as chat rooms) or across time (using asynchronous tools such as discussion boards). In contrast to traditional work situations where people will attend meetings at specific times and block out sections of time for specific activities, participation in a learning community is likely to involve logging into the virtual learning environment and communicating with their peers perhaps several times a week at times to suit the participant.

The literature on time and time management with respect to learning communities, networked learning and communities of practice appears to be sparse and most of the current research is based on e-learning. Salmon (2002) considers the issue of time to be 'emotive and value-laden for both e-moderators and participants'. She discusses how the traditional advantage of anytime and anyplace learning in virtual environments means that time is not bounded or contained as it is when attending traditional lectures or seminars with clearly demarked start and end times. She mentions that e-learning has a reputation for 'eating time' and identifies the importance of being explicit about the time requirements for both participants and e-tutors in e-learning programmes. She emphasizes the importance of being realistic about how much time online activities and communication are likely to take and she also emphasizes that both novice e-learners and e-tutors will need much longer than more experienced participants.

Patterns of access to virtual learning environments in different learning communities

In the past few years we have explored the patterns of access and members' experiences of time in a range of different learning communities, including:

- WISE community, that is a group of professional women returning to employment after a career break;
- steel industry community, that is a group of middle managers working in the steel industry;
- work-based learning community, that is a group of staff involved in delivering work-based qualifications in a university (including academics, colleagues from further education college and colleagues from a primary care health trust);
- networked learning community, that is a group of professional educators taking part in an online Master's programme;
- e-learning community, that is a group of academic, library and ICT staff who came together to develop the e-learning provision within their university;
- a learning community formed to support the implementation of a regional e-learning strategy within the NHS.

In total we explored the time experiences of more than 70 members of these different learning communities. We used a number of different approaches to capture individuals' experiences, including: analysis of postings; use of questionnaires; online and face-to-face discussions; and informal individual and group interviews. Our findings are presented under three main headings:

- Time of access
- Patterns of access
- Community members' metaphors about time.

Time of access

Analysis of community member postings indicates that their access to the online community is dependent on a number of factors. For some members there was little choice as their access was limited to the times when they had access to a computer, for example at work. For individuals with a choice of access, for example work or home, then the times when they accessed the community appear to be partially determined by their perception of the community and its role in their life. Some individuals clearly considered their community membership as a 'work' activity, while others considered it to be for their 'personal development' and/or as a 'social' activity. Some community members maintained very separate boundaries between their public and private lives, while others (particularly individuals who were self-employed) did not draw such distinct boundaries between different parts of their lives. In response to the question 'Why do you choose these times?' people responded:

> They suit me. Other jobs are done, the house is quiet, the phone bill will be less, my brain is relatively active.

> To fit in with my lifestyle. So for example, if I wake up very early on a morning I might log in then. Alternatively, if I'm working to a deadline I might work very late at night. Another time I might have 2 hours free during the day at work. It's the time I have a moveable space.

> Convenience.

> I actually prefer to access the virtual learning community in my personal time, when I know that I will not get interrupted. I am one of those (sad?) individuals who hardly ever watch TV (3 hours a week max) but spend huge amounts of time tinkering with computers and using the internet (up to 14 hours per week). The overriding factor is the weather, if the weather is nice I fly aircraft, if the weather is bad I use the computer.

Clear differences were identified between the access patterns of different communities, for example the women returners demonstrated high levels of access from both work and home and this was in contrast to the managers in the steel industry where access was primarily from work. This difference in access patterns is interesting as the professional women were clearly exploring and expanding their work and social boundaries and, in general, didn't consider their community as solely 'work'. Indeed, an analysis of their messages suggests that more than 80 per cent of the content was social. However, informal interviews with these women suggest that their online communications played a crucial role in helping them to feel supported during a period of change in their lives. Their access patterns demonstrated a mixing of 'work' and family time, that is public and private lives and the contents also demonstrated this mixing, for example many of the women's postings included a mixture of comments on 'work' and family life.

In contrast to the women returners' community, the managers at the steel works tended to perceive their online activities as 'work'. Their pattern of access was predominately work-based and their comments, for example in the questionnaires, and in focus group interviews, confirm this perspective. The managers often shared humour within the virtual community but very few comments related to their home life and 96 per cent of the postings were directly related to work activities. The managers used the discussion board to share good practice, explore work problems and discuss issues related to the working learning community.

The statistical data available from most virtual systems can be a really useful tool in helping facilitators to track community member participation patterns and can inform facilitator judgements about how individuals are coping with community activity.

For example, the Blackboard VLE provides information to facilitators and instructors on:

- total number of accesses per area;
- number of accesses over time;
- user access per hour of the day;
- user accesses per day of the week;
- total accesses by user.

The statistical breakdown of number of accesses over time provided really useful information on the participants' online habits. The statistical data can provide feedback of a surprising kind. Data was collected during week six of a VLC which focused on the topic of facilitating online learning communities. Eleven o'clock in the morning proved to be the most popular time, with 1685 hits during the first six weeks of the community programme, yet members had accessed 9 times at 3 a.m., 27 times at 5 a.m., and 55 times at 6 a.m.! The facilitator was left in no doubt of the commitment of the participants to the programme. The user access per day of the week data provided further useful information. Saturdays were very low participation days yet many of the community were active on Sundays. Monday is the most active day of the week and this tended to be the day when the facilitator outlined plans for the forthcoming week.

In the work-based learning tutor community participant patterns of access were much less cohesive, this seemed to reflect the diversity of the participants themselves. A few participants accessed the programme from home, some notable postings between 10.30 and 12.00 p.m. on Saturday night! Significantly the university academics accessed the community during 'office hours' or in the early evening. Follow-up investigations revealed that academics tended to access the community at the end of the working day from their office rather than home. Colleagues from the further education sector were more flexible in their approach and accessed during the working day and during the evenings, although never at weekends. In contrast the

Primary Care Trust participants only accessed the learning community out-side working hours.

It is clear that anyone who is considering establishing a learning community should clarify whether or not members will be taking part during their work or home time. If they are going to take part during their working day then they will need a time allowance for this activity, it is likely that this will need to be negotiated with their managers and employing organizations.

The participants from the NHS e-learning strategy implementation group identified the allocation of protected time for online activity as a real issue within the NHS. The participants felt that this was so important that they created a discussion thread in the social area to discuss the issue in more detail. Some of their concerns raise important issues for all organizations considering promoting the development of the learning community model, in this case the participants are trainers and training managers thinking of using the learning community model to support dynamic learning and training across the NHS in the North and East Yorkshire and North Lincolnshire region (see Box 9.1).

Box 9.1   Example: Online discussion on the issue of time

Hello
I would be very interested to hear others' thoughts on the issue of 'protected time' for participation in learning communities, as it raises various issues for staff, their line managers and course attendance, etc.

If 2–3 hours a week is say a reasonable estimate of the time needed for this type of learning, perhaps it could be done in chunks which are spread across the week rather than all in one block. The reduction in travelling time and costs to attend sessions in person would no doubt be an advantage here?
Yours Jane

Hi,
I feel quite strongly that there are numerous benefits in pursuing e-learning for some staff training needs. My main reservation, is that Managers or employing organizations will see e-learning as a means of delivering training and development in a quicker and more cost effect-ive manner to the detriment of a positive learning experience. I hope to influence management to see that staff who wish to engage in e-learning and online communities need to be given dedicated/ protected learning time and hope they will ensure this is undertaken in a location where they are undisturbed and can benefit from the course they are undertaking. I would not like to think that somebody is trying to complete a course and is continually trying to answer phones, carry out their daily tasks or being disturbed/disrupted whilst 'learning'.

I think it's important for learners to negotiate time with line managers. It's not as if they have to be online for hours at a time, it could be just 10 minutes, or half-an-hour and surely this could be agreed between the manager and the learner say at the beginning of every week? They could then go online during working hours when it fits in with other demands and as the manager has agreed to this, it would be protected time. I don't think there's any need for time in lieu, as it can be done at work, with a bit of reading as well as online activity. I think if people choose to go online at home, on top of what's been agreed with their line manager, then that's up to them. The hope is that learners will be given protected time during working hours, but it still takes up less time, because they don't have to leave the workplace to attend a course.
Ben

Patterns of access

The findings of an earlier study (Allan 2002) identified three patterns of access: planned; planned and opportunistic; and opportunistic. Individuals who planned their access tended to block out time (from 15 minutes to 3 hours) for their online activities. In contrast individuals who used an opportunistic approach tended to log-in as and when they had the opportunity. These people often logged in several times a day for brief periods. There appears to be an almost equal spread of these three patterns between community participants. Face-to-face and asynchronous discussions about time, and also planned and opportunistic approaches generated much interest from members and for many of them this framework clearly resonated with their personal experiences. Community members who participated in discussions on the theme of time management in face-to-face sessions identified the value of this experience and said that it had enabled them to review and change their approaches to time, for example one person said that she intended to plan her online sessions using her diary as her previous approach of waiting for gaps in the day didn't work.

The topic of time management arose spontaneously in many of the communities considered in our research. Members reflected on time in their asynchronous discussions and an analysis of the number of postings referring to time-related issues showed that they were most prevalent early in the life of the community. This is demonstrated in the graph in Figure 9.1 showing the total number of postings, the number of postings where participants reflected on time, and also the number of postings where community members managed their time, for example arranged chat sessions, face-to-face meetings, etc.

This finding appears to be linked to an individual's need to sort out the tensions associated with managing their time for their online activities. The

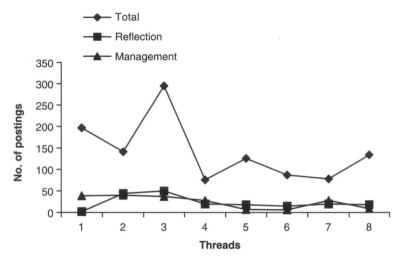

Figure 9.1   Graph showing the pattern of postings in which members reflected on their time management

number of spontaneous discussions on the theme of time-related issues appear to indicate that the issue of time is an important component of a member's experience. In all the learning communities there was a continuous level of activity related to time management where members planned and made arrangements for activities such as face-to-face meetings or synchronous sessions. The postings relating to these conversations were neutral in tone. While it is clear that membership of a virtual community does involve negotiating and planning group activities, this didn't appear to cause any problems or issues with the participants.

Community members' metaphors about time

A simple tool for exploring time-related issues is the use of and analysis of metaphor. Our study also involved an exploration of the metaphors about time used in the postings of members of three of the communities. All the metaphors found in the study could be grouped under one of the following headings:

- time as a scarce commodity;
- challenges in managing time;
- conflict between natural patterns and external factors;
- lack of control.

Time as a scarce commodity, for example:

Problems included – Lack of **time**, adoption of the late 20th century 30-second-attention-span-click-and-download culture.

In particular because in this early stage it seems that I only have **time** to login, quickly read the messages and run – not how I would like it to be!

I too am having difficulty finding enough **time** to do anything other than 'read the messages and run', and it is not through any lack of enthusiasm or interest, I'm just too darn busy at the moment. I'm hoping things will get slightly less busy soon.

Like A and B I have only managed to scrape together enough **time** over the last week to enter WebCT, despair at the number of new postings in the discussion area, and by the **time** I've read through the postings it's **time** to get on with something else. It feels very intimidating to try to put in my views when so much has been said already.

Things are already starting to get a little quieter now, and I am trying to 'make up for lost **time**'.

There is no **time** to reflect . . .

I keep running out of **time**.

Challenges in managing time, for example:

I find the same problems as some of you, in scheduling a regular **time** slot to do justice to the activity.

It's a problem planning a **time** when you can access the environment and getting into a routine and sticking to it.

I think this is a great opportunity to reflect on my own **time** management skills (or lack of them!). I see it as another part of my overall workload not additional take it or leave it because I have made a commitment to the course. The issue is self-discipline for me as it is with all my **time** management issues.

Conflict between natural patterns and external factors, for example:

In particular, whilst I like to work at my own pace I'm finding it difficult to schedule **time** for this – a situation exacerbated because I don't have a PC and Web access at home and I guess I've always been a night owl . . . .

Lack of control, for example:

The timing hampered us a lot I think – the run up to Christmas is always a mad **time** and people just don't have the space to suddenly start working on a project like this. Because of other commitments I think the group found it hard to get going on anything constructive – we spent a lot of **time** just trying to find out if we could all talk together let alone work together.

It's much easier to plan time management **not** using computers. Using the internet, e-mails, etc. was either addictive or time consuming.

The use of these metaphors indicates that these community members experienced a wide range of time challenges. The metaphors indicate that they take a traditional 'clock' approach to time (not surprising given that they all worked in traditional organizations, roles and professions) and their experiences of time were similar to traditional time management perspectives.

Our findings are summarized in Box 9.2.

Box 9.2   Summary of findings

1.   Different people will have a different relationship or approach to time and time management.
2.   Two approaches to time are clock or calendar time (through time) and experiential time (in time).
3.   Individuals will have their own preference to their approach to time and this will vary according to their context.
4.   Online communications support synchronous events that require a clock/calendar approach to time and asynchronous processes that involve either clock/calendar or experiential approaches to time.
5.   Individuals may access their community from work or home and this may indicate their perception of the community – 'work', personal development, leisure.
6.   Individuals may use one of three distinct time management patterns for accessing their online community: planned, opportunistic, mixed (planned and opportunistic).
7.   The metaphors individuals use in their postings indicate their experiences with respect to time.
8.   The metaphors used by community members could be grouped under the following headings: Time as a scarce commodity; Challenges in managing time; Conflict between natural patterns and external factors; and Lack of control.

Overcoming time barriers to active participation

As a designer or facilitator of an online community there are various approaches that you may wish to take to help community members overcome potential time barriers to active participation. You will need to consider the issue of time throughout the community life cycle and particularly at the following phases:

- foundation;
- induction;
- incubation.

Once the learning community is well established then time appears to become less of an issue for individual members.

At the foundation phase of the learning community it is important to think about and discuss the likely time commitments with the design team, facilitators and other stakeholders. It is worthwhile thinking through and gaining agreement from directors and senior managers that the development of a learning community within the organization will involve time and, in the early days, it may involve substantial amounts of time by both members and the facilitator(s). It can be difficult to estimate the amount of time that is involved in active participation within a learning community and, in our experience, it is likely to involve several hours a week, although this will be distributed over the week in relatively short time periods. However, once you have identified the likely time commitment then it is worthwhile making this explicit. You will need to publicize it in all marketing or explanatory materials. It is an issue that is worthwhile raising and covering at any induction event or process too.

As a result of our experiences with learning communities where time was clearly an issue for many participants, we now build in time to enable new community members to reflect on and adapt their time management strategies. The timing of this is important and we found it works well in the early stages of the community life, for example during the induction and incubation phases and once the members have gained some experience of working together in an online community. We have explored this issue with community members in both face-to-face workshops and also through online discussions.

Face-to-face workshops held in the early stages of the life of a community offer an excellent opportunity to explore members' concerns, fears and issues. We have found that an open session on 'concerns, fears and current issues' will often raise the issue of time and provide a space for it to be discussed. This type of session may be structured in a number of different ways:

- **Small group work** Ask people to work in groups of three or four and give them 10 minutes to identify their concerns, fears and current issues. At the end of the 10-minute period ask each group to feed back their findings to the whole group. Write these up on a flipchart or whiteboard. Then lead a discussion on ways of overcoming or resolving the issues.
- **Whole group session** Briefly introduce the issue of time and time management, and explain its importance to active participation in the learning community (about 5 minutes). Hand out the time management questionnaire (Box 9.4 at the end of this chapter) and ask members to complete it. This normally takes about 10 minutes. Once everyone has completed the questionnaire then lead a discussion about the issues that

it has raised. You may want to end this discussion by asking everyone to agree a personal action plan. We find that it is useful if participants write down their intention on a Post-it note to take away with them.

The issue of time may also be explored in online discussion using either a discussion board or chat room. It is worthwhile introducing 'time' during the induction stage of a community where members may, as part of an online introduction activity, state how often they intend to go online. This helps everyone to think about their level of participation in the community. This may then be followed up by introducing a discussion (either asynchronous or synchronous) where you raise the issue of time and online communications. In our experience a simple message asking participants about their experiences results in a deluge of messages. A sample message is shown in Box 9.3.

Box 9.3   Sample message

Subject: Time and participating in the community

Hello everyone,
The community has now been 'live' for four weeks and is quite lively! Experience in other communities suggest that sometimes members experience tensions and issues around time, balancing their workload and their online community activities. I thought it would be useful to introduce this issue and to open up a thread for discussions and comments about your experiences of time. Do feel free to respond to this message with any thoughts or comments that you have on the topic.
Regards
Jim

In addition, you may want to use the questionnaire at the end of this chapter in Box 9.4 as an online tool for facilitating reflection and discussion on this issue.

Activities may also be used to help community members develop the habit of engaging in their community. Synchronous activities such as guest presentations or chat room sessions may be built into the early life of the community. This will help members to develop the habit of taking part in community activities. In the early days, as a facilitator, you may decide to follow up people who haven't yet participated in the community using phone calls or informal meetings.

Finally, members will only find the time to participate if they are benefiting from the community. As soon as they perceive that they are not gaining from their participation then they may leave the community or go underground as evidenced in the following quotation:

Box 9.4   Time and e-learning

The purpose of this questionnaire is to enable you to reflect on the issue of time and your membership of this online community.

General approaches to time

1. How would you describe your general approaches to time?

Time and your participation in the online community

2. Do you normally schedule your virtual sessions, for example write it in a diary, keep set times available?
3. Please comment on your experiences of the differences (if any) between how you intend to access the virtual environment and what actually happens.
4. Do you access the virtual environment opportunistically, for example when you have small pockets of time between other activities, as a result of cancelled meetings, etc.?
5. What do you think the overall balance of your scheduled vs opportunistic use of the virtual environment, for example 10:90, 50:50, 90:10 or any other ratio that reflects your experiences?
6. Please outline any new or different time management issues you have experienced during your involvement with the community.
7. What time management advice would you give to someone joining a virtual community for the first time?

Access to ICT and the virtual environment

Please tick the responses that most match your experiences.

8. I normally use: computer at work ❑
    computer at home ❑
    mixture of work/home computers ❑
    other, for example public library, cyber café ❑
9. On a weekly basis I tend to log into the virtual community:
    0–3 times ❑
    4–7 times ❑
    more than 7 times ❑
10. How long do you tend to stay online each time you log into the virtual community?
    up to an hour ❑
    1–2 hours ❑
    more than 2 hours ❑
11. How long to you tend to work offline, for example reading and preparing messages?:
    up to an hour ❑

1–2 hours ❑
more than 2 hours ❑
12. On a weekly basis how much time do you spend on other community-related activities?
up to an hour ❑
1–2 hours ❑
more than 2 hours ❑
13. Any other comments you would like to make about your experiences as a community member and time management.

The core group goes underground
After months of meeting regularly to discuss cutting-edge problems, a community of six senior engineers grew rapidly. The six senior engineers reluctantly welcomed these newcomers but within a month found that the informal discussion had shifted from cutting edge topics to more basic ones. The community no longer met their needs. One week, much to everyone's surprise, the six senior engineers were missing. After some research, we discovered that they had gone underground, meeting in a separate conference room at the same time.

(McDermott 2000: 19)

Recommendations for community members

1. Allocate time for your online activities. Block small amounts of time out in your diary and be prepared to log in at additional times, for example if there is an unexpected space in your diary.
2. Allocate time for other community activities, for example reading, working on projects. Schedule these in your diary.
3. If your community membership is directly related to your work role or career development then negotiate time off for your online and other activities and/or an adjustment to your workload.
4. Be prepared to make adjustments to your time management habits as you get to grips with participating in a community. Be flexible.

Recommendations for community developers and facilitators

1. Consider the members when you are designing and developing the community. Think through the likely time commitments. Remember that online communications have the potential to 'eat up' time and think about how this can be minimized.
2. Clearly identify the likely time commitments of community membership. Make them explicit. Ensure that these are highlighted in all marketing or explanatory materials.

3. Build in time to enable new community members to reflect on and adapt their time management strategies. The timing of this is important and it is suggested that it happens in the early stages of the community's life, for example initiation and interaction stages once the members have gained some experience of online work.
4. Build in synchronous activities early on in the life of the community. This will help members to develop the habit of taking part in community activities.
5. In the early days follow up people who don't participate, using phone calls or face-to-face meetings wherever possible.

Recommendations for employers

1. Ensure that staff taking part in virtual communities have access to the appropriate ICT.
2. Ensure that staff have time to participate in community activities.
3. Introduce protected time for e-learning and community activities.

10

Working in Partnership

Introduction

The purpose of this chapter is to explore the benefits of developing a virtual learning community as a means of facilitating and supporting strategic partnerships. Partnership working often involves people coming together in multi-professional teams often from different organizations or sectors. This way of working can be extremely demanding and individuals and organizations may experience steep learning curves as they get to grips with the need to understand the differing perspectives and practices of other organizations, teams and individuals. Although partnership working is normally mediated through face-to-face meetings, the development and use of learning technologies can provide a focus and channel for individual and team learning throughout the life of the partnership.

This chapter will explore the use of virtual learning communities as a tool for supporting partnership working and it will focus on the following themes:

- Context for working in partnership.
- Benefits and challenges of working in partnership.
- Effective partnerships.
- Successful partnerships using virtual learning communities.
- Virtual partnerships and project management.

Context for working in partnership

> . . . partnership is one of the most complex and difficult ways in which to work. When it works even reasonably well, however, it can bring some of the best results for the end-user . . .
>
> (Dakers 2003: 47)

Partnership working has achieved a high profile in the past decade as it is seen as a way of meeting the agenda for modernization to improve perform-ance and services in a complex and rapidly changing environment. Sullivan and Skelcher (2002) highlight the rise in collaborative working between public, private and the voluntary and community sectors and they map out how collaboration is central to the way in which public policy is being made, managed and delivered in the UK. The current UK government is intro-ducing policy to promote partnership working as an important strategy for tackling complex and inter-linked problems such as crime, education, health and housing in our inner cities. The new NHS Teaching Trusts are an example of this, for example 'The Black Country Strategy' partnership pro-posed between the University of Birmingham Medical School and six Health Authorities in the region has been formed to address the critical shortages of doctors in the West Midlands. Another example is in the SureStart projects mentioned below (see Box 10.1).

Some partnerships are formed to overcome geographical barriers and boundaries and these may be located across regions or countries or continents (see Box 10.2).

Box 10.1   Example: European Union

The European Union has supported an extensive range of regional collaborative projects which have been funded under a range of initia-tives. One significant example is the Telematics for Libraries pro-gramme that supported 87 main projects and involved more than 350 parties, of whom half were libraries. The Telematics projects produced a variety of outputs and notable examples which have had a significant impact on the library and information community and include the standards such as UNIMARC and EDIFACT and also freeware tools. See http://www.cordis.lu/libraries/. The Telematics programme involved the use of an extensive range of virtual communication tools and a number of virtual learning communities developed in response to the challenges of working in partnership at a distance.

Box 10.2   Example: SureStart

SureStart is a UK government initiative aimed at ensuring that under 5s and their families have easy access to a wide range of support services. SureStart projects are based in areas of social deprivation and each project team is made up of staff from different agencies such as health, social services, lifelong learning (including public libraries) as well as voluntary sector organizations. Managers working on SureStart pro-jects need to quickly develop the necessary infrastructure to provide a variety of family-centred services involving teams of midwives, childcare workers, literacy workers and others.

One of the authors has experience of working with managers from a number of different SureStart projects. She found that they work in a very challenging environment and their day-to-day working life is hectic with massive workloads and the need to respond to a variety of situations from their customers and staff. At the same time this government-funded initative must be responsive to the changing requirements from their funders. These managers, even when working in the same building as each other, find it extremely hard to meet up and reflect and learn from their current practice. One strategy for tackling this situation is that they arrange regular management development days and half days that are held at an external venue and facilitated by an external consultant. These events provide a process whereby they can reflect on current issues and develop new working practices. In between these events the managers can use virtual communication tools to explore and discuss current issues. Their choice of a virtual communication tool is e-mail as this provides simple and easy desktop access to each other. Individual managers have developed different practices with respect to accessing and using their e-mail distribution list. Some use it during their working day whereas others only access it from their home computer. Keeping in regular contact with each other means that they have developed a very simple virtual learning community that augments and supports their face-to-face meetings.

Benefits and challenges of working in partnership

There are many benefits to working in partnership; some are listed below:

- Enhanced access to people, resources and organizations.
- Enhanced ownership – partnerships that are set up to tackle specific problems collaboratively are owned by the partners and this means that the project outcomes are more likely to be accepted and owned by the partner organizations.
- Enhanced quality – the involvement of a wide range of people who bring their different professional perspectives can enhance the quality of the partnership experience and outcomes. Individual partners may be more willing to take on new ideas and working practices as a result of the collaboration.
- Increased exposure to new ideas/approaches – working in multi-professional teams can help partners to broaden their outlook and obtain a broader perspective on issues related to their work and their context.
- Improved use of resources – partnership working can enhance access to resources and also more efficient use of resources.
- Enhanced motivation – being part of a successful partnership can boost

morale and help individuals to develop new enthusiasm for their work. However the opposite may also be true too!
- Continuous professional development – working collaboratively can provide individual workers with the opportunity to develop their knowledge and skills-learning opportunities for the different partners as the result of 'enforced' reflection on individual perspectives and working practices in comparison with those of partners.

Despite the undoubted benefits of working in partnership, there are many challenges to working in and leading collaborative teams or partnerships. The challenges to successful partnership working may be the result of:

- long-held rivalries or competition;
- different values and beliefs;
- power struggles;
- differing perceptions/perspectives;
- potential commitment of large amounts of time, resources and energy;
- differences in systems and procedures;
- differences in organizational cultures;
- conflict due to Intellectual Property Rights;
- restrictions due to professional or organizational confidentiality issues;
- responses of people or organizations NOT involved in the partnership.

As will be seen later in this chapter the key to successful partnership working involves effective partnership management. Developing effective relationships appears to be vital to the success of partnerships and these require a robust framework of communication processes. Meetings, phone calls and printed materials are a basic requirement for the partnership process. In addition, virtual communication tools, for example VLEs, video conferences, virtual conferences, mail groups and at a simple level e-mail enable partners to maintain regular communications with each other and can support the development of virtual learning communities and new approaches to resolving some of the challenges of partnership working.

The following example (Box 10.3) demonstrates how virtual communication tools are being used to support partnership working and communication.

Box 10.3   Project Chrysalis

Ian Everall, Association West Midlands Libraries Challenge Chair, explains the overall purpose of the Challenge Project is to 'create advantage for the region and connect people to opportunity by unlocking the potential values of the strategic assets held within the library sector'. The Challenge Project is made up of a series of projects each involving different partnerships and one of these is the Chrysalis Project. The West Midlands Higher Education Association – Libraries Group (WMHEA–LG), consisting of twelve Higher Education organizations led this project in partnership with University of

Birmingham and Staffordshire and Stoke public libraries. Chrysalis developed a content repository and online materials to support learning and skills developments for use by students, public and private organizations and local communities across the West Midlands region. One of the authors was involved in this project and the development of web-based learning materials on the theme of evaluating web-based information sources. The project manager who was part of the e-learning team led the project and managed a mixture of face-to-face and virtual activities. She set the tone of the project and enabled partners to work together in a collaborative climate. Project partners learnt from each other in a variety of ways, for example colleagues in public libraries shared their knowledge of lifelong learners and the needs of learners with disabilities while colleagues in the universities shared their technical knowledge and also experience of working with diverse groups of undergraduate learners. While the project outcomes included a completed website with diagnostic tool, guide, self-assessment questionnaires and checklist, it also included 'softer' outcomes, that is sharing of knowledge and expertise between different partners and the development of a new community of practice.

Processes of working in partnership

Sullivan and Skelcher (2002) identify and explore different ways of conceptualizing the processes of working in partnership, for example as a life cycle and as a social process. Their life cycle for partnerships is based on the development of collaboration as a series of consecutive stages:

1. Pre-conception – the potential partners, agencies and individuals become aware of the possibility of working in partnership and the potential benefits and needs to do so.
2. Initiation – individuals come together and explore the potential of working together in partnership.
3. Formalization – the partnership is formalized by implementing an appropriate governance structure and/or committing to a project bid.
4. Operation – the project is put into action and partners work together to achieve the project goals.
5. Termination – the project closes or transforms itself into another venture.

This model provides a useful template for exploring and facilitating collaborative arrangements and its structure is similar to that of the stages of the life of a learning community (see Chapters 4, 5 and 6) as shown in Table 10.1.

As with the learning community life cycle, the partnership life cycle model is perhaps an over-simplification. Some potential partnerships will not move

Table 10.1 Comparison of the life cycle of a virtual learning community and that of a partnership

Life cycle of the partnership	Life cycle of a virtual learning community
Preconception – The potential partners, agencies and individuals become aware of the possibility of working in partnership and the potential benefits and needs to do so	At this stage it is unusual for virtual learning communities to be considered as an approach to supporting a partnership
Initiation – Individuals come together and explore the potential of working together in partnership **Formalization** – The partnership is formalized by implementing an appropriate governance structure and/or committing to a project outline or bid	**Initiation** – The concept of using virtual communication tools and perhaps developing a virtual learning community may be raised here. It may be written into the project outline or bid
Operation – the project is put into action and partners work together to achieve the project goals	**Induction** – Individuals join the project and are introduced to it and working online **Incubation** – Socialization. Information exchange **Improving performance** – Starts work on real-life problems. Collaborative and cooperative work. Development and testing of new practice/products. Feedback **Implementation** – Transfer of ideas and practice into the workplace
Termination – The project closes or transforms itself into another venture	**Closure or transformation** – The end of the project and perhaps partnership. The learning community is no longer required and is either formally ended or it may fizzle out. It may be replaced by another community with different focus/membership

beyond the preconception stage and many stall at the initiation stage. Others may transform into a new initiative during the formalization stage when individuals develop a better understanding of their context and the project potential. However, this model used in association with the virtual community life cycle model does help to provide facilitators with guidance on how to manage the process of working in partnership. The extended case study in Box 10.4 illustrates some of the realities of working in partnership and the wide range of activities that need to take place to ensure that it is successful. In addition, it illustrates how it took almost a year to establish a strong and effective partnership.

Box 10.4   Case study: Cooperation in public and scientific libraries in Denmark: Net Librarian project

Vera Daugaard (2003) describes the cooperative partnership which brought together Danish public and scientific librarians and now involves more than 150 librarians. The aim of the partnership project was to provide easier access to the scientific libraries' knowledge and resources for the general public and the amateur researcher using the internet. Daugaard writes 'The advantages of establishing a co-operation were obvious for both parties and consequently – in August 2002 – a joint project between the public libraries and four scientific libraries was launched as a pilot with a view to developing a model for the future co-operation. Denmark's Electronic Research Library (DEF) provided funding for the establishment and the pilot ran until the end of the year 2002.'

Daugaard (2003: 2) identifies some of the barriers to partnership working and these included:

Technical barriers

- Firewalls – the use of different firewalls by the collaborating libraries caused technical problems.
- Simple hardware – staff needed support in using a range of technical equipment.

Practical barriers

- Lack of non-written communications in the enquiry process.
- The enquiry form – readers did not want to complete a long form and answer too many 'personal questions'.
- Providing written answers was time-consuming for librarians.

Mental barriers

- Different corporate cultures in the 34 cooperating libraries.
- Lack of privacy – individual communications with readers were now open to all librarians to read and staff were not used to being 'looked at in that way'.
- Local pride and competition between libraries. The desire to 'show off' your professional skills.
- Lack of knowledge of the individual reader who may not be from your local community.
- Fear of losing local resources – some librarians were afraid that management would cut local resources if Net Librarian was successful.

- Using Net Librarian prevented readers from developing their own information skills and so was in conflict with current library practices of providing user education and then expecting the reader to carry out the searches themselves.
- Reduction in people visiting the library. Some librarians believed that the patrons should visit the physical library and so they supplied answers which directed people to visit the library and borrow books.
- Lack of ownership to Net Librarian – it took time for librarians to feel that Net Librarian was part of 'their' library.

The partners used a range of initiatives to overcome these barriers and these included: face-to-face meetings; a project manual; and the use of a mailing list. The mailing list enabled the librarians involved in Net Librarian to participate in discussions about working in Net Librarian, to share common problems and queries, and to provide help and support for each other. It provided a means by which a virtual learning community developed.

The Net Librarian service required library staff to work together and develop an independent organization, New Librarian, with its own identity. This identity was developed through staff training, the artefacts of the new service (website, manuals, etc.) and also the mailing list.

Overall, the project has been successful, and Daugaard (2003: 8) writes:

> Despite some difficulties arising in this co-operation process, they are greatly outweighed by the advantages. Both parties had some preconceived ideas about each other and each others' institutions. But these myths have slowly, but surely been demolished over the past 9 months, and through our common project we have gained insight into each others' ways of working, built up a well-functioning network and learned to respect each others' qualities and competencies. We are in no doubt whatsoever that through this common inquiry service we are able to exploit the resources far better, both in terms of materials and competencies – to the benefit and joy of the Danish citizens.

Effective partnerships

What are the pitfalls in partnership working? Different partners will have different starting points in terms of: their experience, confidence and competence in collaborative work; their technical skills and know-how; their financial resources; and their ability to commit to the partnership's purpose. If one dominant partner takes over then this can lead to resentment by other members and they may ultimately withdraw from the project. If a small number of people take on the majority of the work then this can lead to them feeling resentful as they are 'carrying' other team members. It can also mean that other team members begin to lose ownership of the purpose or outcome. If credit and accountability is not shared by the whole partnership then this can weaken it and also cause conflict. This may cause long-term breakdowns in relationships, meaning that future partnership working is at risk.

Making partnerships work well involves individuals and particularly partnership leads, facilitators and managers investing time for building and maintaining the relationships and partnership processes. This requires sensitivity to the culture and working practices of others, and also an ability to work in a flexible way that involves everyone in 'give and take'. Colin Harris (2002) says that one of the main drawbacks of collaborative working is that it is extremely time-consuming. Time is required for: joint working and decision making; keeping partners informed; identifying and resolving differences in working practices between different organizations; travel to meetings at different locations; joint report writing and dissemination activities. Working in partnership can add another level of bureaucracy to the task in hand. Working through the different procedures and working practices of organizations (or even departments within the same organization) can be extremely time-consuming and stultifying. It often leads to the need for many meetings and usually requires careful documentation of agreements.

Successful partnerships using virtual learning communities

There are many different approaches to organizing a partnership. One approach is to have a single project manager who has overall responsibility for the purpose of the partnership and who works with a team of individuals distributed across different departments or organizations. Another approach is to share responsibility between the partner organizations, with each partner organization providing an identified lead person. The example in Box 10.5 illustrates one partnership where a project manager was appointed to lead a task group made up of members from different organizations.

Virtual partnerships and project management

Partnerships that become learning communities to focus on the development of a 'project' outcome are likely to need a project manager. The project manager is not necessarily the community facilitator, as we see in the voluntary sector example (Box 10.5), the project manger can be focused on the project outcome while the learning community facilitator will be more focused on the interactions of the community project team. One of the key roles of the facilitator is to create and maintain a 'glue' that holds the partners and project team(s) together. The project 'glue' includes both informal and formal processes and these are outlined in Table 10.2. 'Soft' or

---

Box 10.5   Working in partnership with the voluntary sector

Background

The Humber Learning Consortium (HLC) is an umbrella agency brokering training for all voluntary sector organizations throughout the Humber region. Representatives from the HLC invited colleagues in the Centre for Lifelong Learning at the University of Hull to form a partnership to address the need for workforce development focusing on the professional development needs of managers in the voluntary sector. The following model was developed.

The HLC appointed a project manager to lead the initiative from the HLC and the University of Hull identified a programme leader, with a background in generic management skills and a commitment to innovation and establishing new ways of working. A task group was formed including staff from the HLC, experienced voluntary sector trainers and staff from the University of Hull, this task group became a learning community. The agreed aim of the learning community was to design a 60 credit University Certificate for Voluntary Sector Managers. One of the first jobs that the task group faced was to agree roles and responsibilities for the HLC project manager and the university programme leader.

The following points were agreed: the role of the HLC project manager was to act as a link person between the HLC and the tutors and the university. He was also responsible for the following activities:

- Liaising with the university and participating in the formative and summative review of the evaluation process.
- Marketing the programme.
- Recruitment of programme participants.
- Liaising with tutors when problems occur.
- Liaising with the LSC and securing programme funding.
- Supporting and guiding participants with practical help and advice.
- Maintainig links with HLC colleagues.

The university programme director's responsibilities include:

- Ensuring that the programme complies with university regulations re: quality assurance.
- Providing support for the VLE.
- Liaising with the HLC on all aspects of the programme.
- Room bookings and accommodation at the university.
- Monitoring and reviewing programme delivery.
- The administration of programme and module examination boards.
- Support for the tutors.
- Monitoring module assessments.

The members of the task group learning community used the Blackboard VLE to support their communications in between the face-to-face curriculum planning meetings. Use of virtual communication tools was embedded into the curriculum development process. The VLE provided an infrastructure to support a new approach to curriculum design, the participants worked as a collaborative learning community and traditional barriers between work-based practitioners and academics were broken down. Module and programme specifications were exchanged, amended and adapted through the virtual learning environment. Task group members commented on each others' suggestions and an open forum was established where all those involved in the development were able to express their views and opinions on work-based assessment strategies and innovative flexible teaching and learning approaches focusing on action learning sets.

The programme has now been granted university approval and the programme director (University of Hull academic) will support the voluntary sector trainers in delivering the programme using blended face-to-face and online learning and teaching modes. The community of practice approach modelled through the collaborative curriculum design working partnership has been embedded into the learning and teaching strategy for the programme. Effective knowledge transfer between the university on e-learning pedagogy, generic management skills and quality assurance and the voluntary sector on the skills gaps in their profession, knowledge and understanding of sector-specific management issues and long-standing experience of training in the voluntary sector was achieved. This collaborative partnership approach to curriculum design was successful and neither of the partners could have produced the final agreed programme independently.

Table 10.2 Types of project 'glue'

Soft	Hard
• shared goals(s) • shared values and beliefs • common concerns and deeper convictions • meetings and social networking • informal communications, e.g. e-mail or phone calls • informal feedback • goodwill • people – such as project managers and project team members	• contracts • terms of reference • memoranda of agreement • service level agreements • project programmes (e.g. Microsoft Project), use of project management tools such as Gantt charts • reporting regimes, e.g. reporting back to senior managers • funding regimes • legal requirements

people-centred approaches include bringing to the surface shared values and beliefs, building on commonality, respecting differences, and learning through informal communication and spending time together. In contrast, 'hard' approaches include legal contracts, terms of reference, agreed working practices, procedures and protocols, and the outputs of project management tools. Both types of project 'glue' are important. If the project comes across barriers or problems that cannot be solved informally then the formal arrangements such as contracts, memoranda of agreements and the documentation of formal meetings become vital tools to help sort out the situation and move the project forward.

Forming virtual learning communities to support partnership projects

As we have already seen in examples such as the Humber Learning Consortium voluntary sector (Box 10.5) and the Chrysalis Project (Box 10.3), virtual communication tools provide a forum for project partners to maintain regular contact with each other between formal meetings and they can help to bond the 'soft' project glue. Communication tools such as e-mail, discussion groups and chat rooms provide a quick and easy communication channel, and they may be used by the project manager or facilitator to establish an interactive learning community. In addition the technical functions of many group communication systems such as LotusNotes mean that the project management and documentation processes can take place in a virtual environment, making vital information accessible to all partners.

How does facilitating a virtual learning community in the partnership context differ from facilitating other communities?

Table 10.1 suggests that virtual learning communities developed in the context of partnership working experience the same life cycle as other learning communities, this is covered in depth in Chapters 4, 5 and 6. At the initiation stage the project manager or facilitator will need to ensure that an appropriate framework for the learning community is established and that an appropriate ICT infrastructure is put in place (see Chapter 3).

The initial stages of the learning community project activity may involve extensive facilitation and management as individuals from differing professional and organizational backgrounds are brought together in a virtual world, and these early stages are probably the most crucial in terms of creating a strong foundation for effective working. The more partners and more complex the project then the greater amount of time and attention to detail needs to be paid to the initial stages. Dakers (2003: 47) identifies that most partnerships significantly underestimate the length of lead time required to set up and run projects when she states 'organisations considering this complex level of collaboration should allow significantly more lead time than for projects with fewer partners. No doubt we will produce the results to time, but all will be somewhat greyer for it.'

Working in partnership is probably best facilitated through a series of face-to-face meetings where partners are involved in induction and incubation activities such as introductions; surfacing expectations, hopes and fears; creating the vision; building the objectives; agreeing the action plan. The process of surfacing expectations is a simple and yet very important one. Asking partners what they expect to get out of the partnership will enable similar and also different expectations to be aired and discussed. It will also help to prevent theoretically small issues becoming inhibitors to the project process. If the partnership is going to include a virtual learning community then it needs to be established at this stage. The authors' experiences suggest that many groups are not aware of the potential advantages of using virtual communication tools and this is often a result of their lack of confidence and experience of using such tools. The project manager or community facilitator may need to introduce the use of e-mail, discussion groups or chat rooms as part of the standard partnership working protocols. In addition they may need to provide some basic information and communications training as discussed in Chapters 3 and 4. As individuals become experienced and familiar with online tools they are then likely to expand their use to include the exchange of information and resources, to problem solve, to discuss underlying tensions and challenges and to move towards the generation of new knowledge and understanding.

Online partners need to experience the benefits of online communication in order to commit to using them, for example, the project manager or facilitator could introduce the use of virtual communication tools as an aid to problem solving. This often happens quite naturally as one member of the community asks a question and others respond, leading to lively online engagement. Once individuals find out that the online community is a source of help, information and encouragement that transcends usual restrictions in time and space then it is likely to take on a life of its own. The value of virtual communications is illustrated in Box 10.6.

Role of the virtual project or partnership manager

Project managers or coordinators who decide to use a virtual learning community as a means of supporting and developing effective project work will be involved in managing technical, project and social aspects of the communications process. This will include managing the following aspects.

Technical

• Ensuring an appropriate virtual communication platform.

Box 10.6   Example: Working on a collaborative digitization project

Cross-institutional project working is common in higher education and other sectors. One learning development worker shared her experiences with the authors.

> I was involved in an externally-funded digitization project that involved partners from higher education, public libraries and the museums services. I found our face-to-face meetings extremely daunting as they were very formal, tightly structured and involved senior staff. Their paperwork was awesome. What made the project come to life for me was our e-mail discussion group. It was here that the real life of the project took place. It was much easier to ask questions within the e-mail group than at meetings and most of them were answered very quickly. We were developing new techniques and procedures and at times it felt as if we were on the cutting edge of digitization. The e-mail group enabled us to quickly pool problems and potential solutions. Overall I learnt a lot from the e-mails and felt much more confident about what I was doing. This could have been because I realized that we were all 'making it up' as we went along. We developed into a small and quite intimate community. Messages were very informal and we quite often shared jokes with each other. One of the members was a director of a library service and he was very helpful to me when I was looking for a new job because I was coming to the end of my contract. I can see from earlier in our meeting that this is an example of a 'learning community'; at the time it felt like a group of helpful and trusted friends.
>
> Sam, Development worker

- Ensuring appropriate technical support.
- Ensuring that the administrative arrangements, for example User IDs and passwords are in place.

Project work

- Overall management of project work.
- Monitoring and controlling tasks and activities.
- Knowledge management.
- Provision of feedback and support to individuals and group(s).
- Offering advice and support with respect to problems.

Social aspects

- Development of an appropriate online working environment.
- Development of friendly, informal communications.

Table 10.3 attempts to identify issues for project managers with the virtual learning community life cycle model. Each stage of the community life cycle is mapped against activities that project managers are likely to be engaged in.

Table 10.3 Project manager or facilitator activities

Life cycle of a virtual learning community activities	*Project manager or facilitator activities*
Initiation – The concept of using virtual communication tools and perhaps developing a virtual learning community may be raised here. It may be written into the project outline or bid	Obtain formal agreement for the development of a learning community Select and establish the information and communications technology infrastructure Establish an appropriate environment with welcome messages, etc. Identify and be ready to implement practical approaches to knowledge management Ensure partners are able to access the technology. Sort out User IDs, passwords, etc.
Induction – Individuals join the project and are introduced to it and working online	Ideally start with introductions, ice-breakers, ground rules, etc. in a face-to-face context. Start off gently with online communications, if appropriate use another round of introductions to help individuals start to develop their online voice. Welcome new team members or late arrivals Provide a structure for getting started, e.g. agreement of group rules, Netiquette Wherever possible avoid playing 'ping-pong' with individual team members and ask other people for their opinions and ideas Encourage quieter team members to join in Where appropriate provide summaries of online discussions
Incubation – Socialization. Information exchange	Provide highly structured activities at the start of the group life Encourage participation Ask questions

	Encourage team members to post short messages
	Allocate online roles to individual members, e.g. to provide a summary of a particular thread of discussion
	Close of threads as and when appropriate
	Archiving of relevant information
	Encourage an informal, positive and constructive atmosphere
Improving performance – Starts work on real-life problems. Collaborative and cooperative work. Development and testing of new practice/ products. Feedback	Facilitate online activities
	Monitor and facilitate the process with respect to project plan
	Ask questions
	Encourage problem solving and trouble shooting
	Encourage reflection
	Identify and record new and developing information and knowledge
	Archive relevant information
	Intervene if there is serious conflict (interventions may be private using phone or a meeting)
Implementation – Transfer of ideas and practice into the workplace	Continue project work
	Obtain feedback of impact on practice
	Encourage problem solving and trouble shooting
	Identify and record new and developing practice
	Monitor and facilitate the process with respect to project plan
Closure or transformation – The end of the project and perhaps partnership. The learning community is no longer required and is either formally ended or it may fizzle out. It may be replaced by another community with different focus/ membership	Ensure 'loose ends' are completed
	Highlight project and partnership achievements
	Encourage (structured) reflection and evaluation on project process
	Thank partners for their contributions and work
	Formally close the project

Summary

Working in partnerships that work well and result in successful project outcomes is an exciting and creative process. They provide opportunities for innovative developments within and across organizations and sectors. Partnership working is extremely challenging and virtual learning communities can provide a dynamic 'space' to support collaborative approaches to learning and development. The project manager may take on the role of learning community facilitator and awareness of the learning community life cycle is likely to enable the project manager to encourage the kinds of activities that will help the 'soft glue' that bonds partners in working together successfully.

11
Evaluation

Introduction

The purpose of this chapter is to explore approaches and issues associated with evaluating virtual learning communities. Evaluation is concerned with establishing a process which results in gathering data and information to enable us to assess the value of a virtual learning community by identifying its outcomes and impact, identifying issues during the process of its life cycle and management. Evaluations may be carried out for a number of different reasons:

- Sponsors and senior managers may want to justify their investment of time and money, and to identify the direct benefits of the learning community to individuals and also the parent organization.
- Managers who have initiated a community may want to identify its impact on their staff and organization.
- The facilitators of the community may want to identify what has worked well and which areas need improvement within the community.
- Researchers who are interested in virtual learning communities may want to evaluate individual communities as a means of developing the knowledge base on this dynamic and evolving way of learning and working.

The evaluation process involves finding answers to questions such as:

- Did the community achieve its outcomes?
- Did the community achieve any unexpected outcomes?
- How did members change their professional practice as a result of their membership of the community?
- How effective were the facilitator(s) in facilitating the community?
- How effective was the ICT infrastructure in supporting the community?
- What was the impact of the community on the rest of the organization?
- What did we learn from the virtual learning community?
- What will we do differently next time?

Planning the evaluation process

It is worthwhile considering who will carry out the evaluation process. Sometimes the evaluation process is carried out by the community facilitator and the obvious disadvantage of this approach is that they are likely to be biased (either intentionally or unconsciously) and stakeholders may find it difficult to provide the facilitator with honest feedback if they know that person well. In many organizations the evaluation process may be carried out by a member of staff with special responsibility for research or quality issues, or it may be carried out by an external evaluator or a consultant.

If the project is externally funded then the funding body or sponsor may require an evaluation. This may be carried out **by** the funder themselves or someone who is contracted by them or it may be carried out by the project team **for** the funder. The funders may be motivated by different reasons, for example to justify their expenditure to their sponsors, to demonstrate the success of the project and its outcomes, and/or to identify areas for improvement (both for themselves as funders and also the project organization). The advantages and disadvantages of independent versus internal evaluators leading the evelution process are summarized in Table 11.1.

Planning the evaluation process is best carried out at the initial stages of the community life as this will enable the necessary data to be collected throughout its life cycle. It involves identifying the principles of the evaluation process and answering questions such as those outlined under the following subheadings.

Overall design principles

- What is the main purpose of evaluating the virtual learning community?
- Who will read and respond to the outcomes of the evaluation process?
- Who will carry out the evaluation process?
- What will be evaluated, for example outcomes of the community, community life process, facilitation of the community, management of the community, technical infrastructure?
- Who will be involved in the evaluation process, for example community members, facilitator(s), workplace colleagues, team leaders and managers' sponsors?
- What resources are available for the evaluation process?

Methods and techniques

- What type(s) of information will be collected?
- How will information be collected – through community records, for

Table 11.1 Leading the evaluation process

Evaluator	Advantages	Disadvantages
Community facilitator or someone closely involved in the community process	Knows the community and its processes Knows the stakeholders Carries out the evaluation as part of their community work	May be biased May not have very good evaluation skills
Colleague from same organization	Understands the context Carries out the evaluation as part of their 'normal' work and doesn't require additional payment Enables them to learn more about virtual learning communities	May be biased May not have very good evaluation skills
Colleague from same organization with specialist role, e.g. researcher, evaluator, quality control	Understands the context Has very good evaluation skills Carries out the evaluation as part of their 'normal' work and doesn't require additional payment Enables them to learn more about the project	May be biased
Consultant or external researcher	Has very good evaluation skills Unbiased Takes additional time to get to understand the virtual learning community and its context Ideally has experience of evaluating a wide range of projects and can bring with them a broader perspective	Takes time to identify appropriate person and ensure that they have the relevant skills May be relatively expensive as needs to be paid in 'real' money May not understand specific context
Funding organization or their representative	May have very good evaluation skills Will bring in an external perspective and experience of evaluating a wide range of projects	May not have very good evaluation skills May focus on a fixed or limited set of evaluation criteria May not understand the context or specific project

example discussion group messages or chat room transcripts, statistical data available through VLEs, questionnaires, interviews, focus groups, observation?

- How will the results be analysed?

Presentation of evaluation

- How will the evaluation be presented?
- Who is the audience?
- How will the findings be disseminated?

Responding to the evaluation

- Who will judge success?
- Who will recommend change?
- Who will be responsible for implementing the recommendations?

There are two main approaches to evaluation:

1. Evaluating the management and administration of a virtual learning community.
2. Evaluating the community and its outcomes.

These are now considered in turn.

Evaluating the management and administration of a virtual learning community

It is worthwhile evaluating the management and administration of the virtual learning community as sometimes problems arising from weak management or administration may have a negative effect on the whole community. This involves asking the types of questions outlined under the following subheadings.

Members

- Have the most appropriate people been invited to join the community?
- Were they provided with appropriate guidance on what to expect?
- Were they supported by their manager?

Facilitators

- How effective were the facilitators in supporting the community?
- Did they have the appropriate level of specialist knowledge and skills?

Administration

- Were the administrative arrangements effective, for example initial letters of invitation, arrangements for meetings, refreshments?

Technology

- Did community members have easy access to the necessary ICT?
- Were the ICT help mechanisms effective?
- Were there any significant ICT problems, for example server crashing? If so, what impact did they have on the community?

Management

- How effective was the steering group/management group in providing leadership for the community?
- Were all appropriate stakeholders involved in the management (and running) of the community?

Evaluating the community and its outcomes

A virtual community may be evaluated at a number of different levels:

- Individual responses to the community.
- Individual learning.
- Development of knowledge.
- Changes in professional practice.
- Impact on parent organization.
- Impact of virtual learning community.

Individual responses to the community

This is concerned with how a member feels about their participation in the community and it is very much a measure of their reaction (at an emotional and intellectual level) to their experiences. Evaluation methods used to identify this type of response include questionnaires, bulletin board discussions, focus group meetings, interviews, for example, face-to-face or using a chat room.

Individual learning

This is concerned with identifying what an individual has learnt from their membership of the community. As with individual responses or reactions, this information may be collected using questionnaires, responses to a posting, focus group meetings, interviews. One challenge in collecting this type of information is identifying what has actually been learnt rather than what someone says they have learnt and, as a result, this type of information is sometimes collected from colleagues or managers.

Development of knowledge

One of the strengths of a virtual learning community is that it encourages the construction and development of new knowledge. How can this be identified? One approach is for the community itself to organize a process for identifying and collating new knowledge and some communities appoint a member as community librarian. Their role is to source the knowledge needed by the community and manage the knowledge generated by the community, that is to support knowledge management. Another approach is for an external person, for example organizational information or knowledge manager, to harvest the new information and knowledge from the community. This means that lessons learnt by the community are not lost and the findings are made available to a much broader community.

Changes in professional practice

What impact has membership of a virtual learning community had on the workplace or individual professional practice? This may be identified through the use of questionnaires, responses to postings, focus group meetings, or interviews. As with individual learning it is a good idea to involve individuals in the workplace in gathering this information.

Impact on parent organization

What impact has the virtual learning community had on the parent organization? How has the community helped the organization to achieve its goals and targets? If the community was clearly aligned with the organization's strategy then it may be possible to identify specific ways in which it has had an impact on the organization's performance.

Impact of virtual learning community

Increasingly it is becoming common to evaluate the impact of any change or innovation such as the implementation of a virtual learning community on stakeholders and Peter Brophy (2002: 2) identifies the potential impact as: 'may be positive or negative (though very often we focus on positive impacts); may be what was intended or something entirely different; may result in changed attitudes, behaviours, products (i.e. what an individual or group produces during or after interaction with the service); may be short or long term; may be critical or trivial.' He describes different 'levels' of impact and lists the following possible responses to a significant change as: hostility; dismissive; none; awareness raised; better informed; improved knowledge; changed perception. It is important to measure the impact of the virtual learning community and to include this in the standard evaluation process.

Methods of evaluation

The evaluation of a virtual learning community involves the use of traditional tools and techniques such as questionnaires and interviews as well as developing approaches, for example narrative analysis of discussion group messages. Table 11.2 provides an overview of some of the tools used in evaluating virtual learning communities.

Once there is clarity about the design principles of the evaluation process then it is important to think about the information requirements and this involves thinking about:

- Who needs the information?
- What information is required?
- How will it be obtained?
- Who are the most appropriate people to collect it?
- How will they collect this information?
- When will they collect this information?
- How will the information be analysed?
- How will it be presented to others?

Virtual learning community statistics will typically make up part of the evaluation process and they may include figures such as:

- Number of members involved in the community.
- Number of member hours involved in the projects.
- Number of postings on the virtual system, for example number of postings per day or week.
- Number and length of recorded chat room sessions.
- Number of hits to the virtual community site.
- Number of postings read.
- Number of accesses to community resources.

Table 11.2 Tools used in evaluating virtual learning communities

	Individual responses to the community	Individual learning	Development of knowledge	Changes in professional practice	Impact on organization	Impact of virtual learning community
Project documentation	*	*	*	*		
Analysis of participation levels in the community, e.g. using software tracking tools	*					
Analysis of narrative in virtual environment	*	*	*	*		
Member questionnaires, reports or learning journals	*	*	*	*	*	
Manager questionnaires or reports		*	*	*	*	*
Customer survey				*	*	*
Stakeholder survey			*	*	*	*
Employer survey			*	*	*	*
Interviews	*	*	*	*	*	*
Focus group	*	*	*	*		
Performance appraisal				*	*	*
Organizational results on performance indicators						
Results on team/unit indicators				*	*	*
Results on personal performance indicators				*	*	*
Top management opinion		*	*	*	*	*

- Number of individual participant contributions.
- Number of facilitator postings.

Community statistics are most easily collected if you know what information you require at the start of the virtual learning community and this enables you to collect this information throughout the life of the community rather than be involved in a major information collecting activity at the end of the project. If the latter occurs then it is possible that you may not be able to collect some of the statistics as they are no longer available. Formal documents and records all provide vital information and, if the structure and format of these are agreed at the start of the community then it can save a lot of time. Many community facilitators keep a reflective diary and this can provide useful information too as it will help capture day-to-day information, ideas and thoughts which may otherwise be lost. Documentation from a help desk is also useful as it can illustrate the number and type of technical queries asked by community members.

Many group communication software packages and also learning environments such as Blackboard or WebCT provide tracking tools which provide basic statistics such as the number of times a member has logged into the system, read messages, responded to messages, etc. This provides vital information as it can be used to illustrate the pattern of activity within a community. Examples of the use of participation statistics from Blackboard were given in Chapter 9. Another useful source of information is the actual messages themselves and transcripts of chat room or conference sessions. These can be downloaded and then analysed as discussed below.

Questionnaires

Questionnaires are a relatively simple method of collecting information but they are deceptively time consuming to design and analyse. Questionnaires generally contain two types of question:

1. Closed questions where there are a limited number of answers, for example yes/no, rating on a scale of 1 to 5.
2. Open questions where the respondent has an opportunity to write their thoughts, ideas or impressions, for example 'What do you think of Service X?', 'How has project Y had an impact on your work?'

Closed questions are relatively simple to analyse and process, while open questions often provide extremely useful information but this may be more challenging to evaluate. Questionnaires may be sent out to individuals via e-mail or post, alternatively individuals may be asked to complete them at service points or in meetings. Increasingly interactive questionnaires are included in online systems and services, and these provide another route for obtaining feedback. Example questionnaires are given in Boxes 11.1

Box 11.1   Sample questionnaire: Evaluation of an induction event

The purpose of this questionnaire is to help us to evaluate the face-to-face learning community induction session. Your feedback will provide us with valuable information.

1.   What did you hope to get out of the induction session?

2.   General comments about the session:

3.   Please indicate your evaluation of the session:
     (Poor = 1, Excellent = 5)

Facilitators		Information provided	
Printed resources		Group discussions	
Activities		WebCT session	

4.   What was the most useful part of the session?

5.   How could the session be improved?

6.   As a result of the induction sessions what are your expectations about becoming a member of the learning community?

7.   Any other comments?

Thank you for completing this questionnaire

and 11.2, and the advantages and disadvantages of questionnaires are summarized in Table 11.3.

Box 11.2   Facilitating learning communities: Evaluation form

Please complete the form anonymously.

Ring the appropriate number or answer and add comments in the spaces provided.

If you need to, please indicate particular workshops, e.g. WS1, WS2 or WS3.

Please return the completed evaluation form to Dina Lewis at the end of the session.

Preparation and support

Individual

1. Were you adequately prepared to participate in this learning community? Please comment:

2. Would you recommend that any other support information should be made available to participants before the beginning of the community? Please comment:

Organizational

3. Have you received adequate support from your organization for your participation in the learning community? Please comment in terms of time release, cover for your post in your absence, etc.

4. How could your organization better support future learning community participants?

Content of the workshops

5. Did the face-to-face workshops match your expectations?

1	2	3	4	5
Not at all				**Very well**

Please comment:

6. What did you think of the facilitator's organization and presentation of material?

1	2	3	4	5
Poor				Excellent

Please comment:

7. Did you feel that you were sufficiently active and involved in the workshops?

1	2	3	4	5
Definitely not				Definitely

Please comment:

8. What did you think about the content of the workshops? Please comment:

9. Were the topics relevant to your needs?

1	2	3	4	5
Not at all				Very

Please comment:

10. Were there any particular strengths or weakness in the facilitator's approaches? Please comment:

11. Do you have any suggestions for improvements in either the content or the presentation of the workshops? Please comment:

12. Do you have any other comments on the workshops?

Online activity

13. Did you enjoy the online activities?

1	2	3	4	5
Not at all				Very much

Please comment:

14. Which activity did you learn most from? And why?

15. What do you think are the advantages and disadvantages of online learning communities?

16. What were the most important learning issues for you? And why?

Impact on your work

17. Do you think that your work-based practice will change as a result of this experience? How?

18. Do think that you have changes as a result of this learning community experience, if so how?

19. Any other comments?

Thank you for completing this form

Interviews

Interviews are an extremely useful way of 'getting beneath the surface' and obtaining detailed information and views from people. As with questionnaires, interviews may involve open or closed questions and they may be structured (where the interviewer asks a set list of questions); semi-structured (where the interviewer provides some prompts or questions, and then follows up individual responses); or unstructured interviews enable the respondent to talk through their ideas and 'go with the flow'. One major disadvantage with interviews is that they can be difficult to arrange as busy people may not want to give up their time. In addition, interviews can be time consuming both to design, take part in, and analyse. We have experimented with online interviews using conferencing or chat software and this appears to be a useful evaluation tool particularly as the ensuing transcript is readable! However, this type of interview does demand that the individuals concerned have access to the technology and are comfortable with its use. Another approach to interviews is to use 'critical event recall' and an application of this technique applied to a virtual learning community is described by Lally (2002b). This technique involved telephone interviews with community participants who had previously read transcripts from their community activities. These transcripts were used during the interview to help them recall and probe their cognitive, affective and social processes that were not expressed within the community. Lally concludes that this is a useful technique that 'can complement content analysis in an important way by using its results to probe "the thinking behind the text" in collaborative

Table 11.3 Advantages and disadvantages of different data gathering techniques

	Advantages	*Disadvantages*
Software tracking tools	Information is available from the system and it is relatively easy to download it and input them into other packages, e.g. word processing or spreadsheets	Information may only be available in a fixed format Software package may offer a limited number of features, e.g. some systems will track who has read each message while others only track total number of readings
Use of discussion group messages or transcripts	Information is readily available and accessible All the messages/ transcripts are date stamped There is no manual transcription of tapes or conversations	Time-consuming to analyse Doesn't provide access to members' private thought processes
Questionnaires	Relatively simple to disseminate A number of different people can be involved in disseminating them and collecting them in	May be time-consuming to design and analyse May be a low return as a result of individuals being unwilling to complete them
Interviews	Provides in-depth information Can follow up new ideas or thoughts	May be time-consuming to design and analyse May be difficult to arrange
Focus groups	Provides in-depth information Individuals may 'spark off' ideas with each other Can follow up new ideas or thoughts	May be time-consuming to design and analyse Data collection methods, e.g. video, audio tape, may be intrusive and put participants off May be difficult to arrange Need an experienced facilitator

work within advanced learning communities in networked environments' (Lally 2002b: 16).

Focus groups are often used as a way of obtaining information from a group of people who come together in a meeting which is facilitated by a researcher. The discussions in these meetings are frequently recorded by audio or video tape and then analysed. The advantages of using a focus group means that the session may be structured, unstructured or semi-structured, individuals have the opportunity to 'spark' ideas off each other and this can lead to extremely rich and fruitful discussions. However, focus groups can be difficult to organize as many people don't have time to attend such a session. In addition, they need careful facilitation so that the facilitator or session leader doesn't introduce bias and, finally, the results of these sessions can be quite time-consuming to analyse.

Analysing information

The community evaluation process involves analysing the information that you obtain and drawing conclusions from your findings. Quantitative information is best analysed using simple statistics and measures such as: mean, mode, average and range. Information is often best presented using graphs and charts which enable the reader to quickly identify trends and themes. Qualitative information is often harder to analyse and the simplest approach is often to identify underlying themes and trends and then present using a simple summary perhaps supported by quotations. The selective use of relevant quotations can help reports to be interesting and they bring out more personal aspects of the experience.

The development of narrative analysis of online discussion groups has become increasingly important in recent years and there are different ways of tackling this. A number of different approaches exist for exploring community activities including:

- analysing the content of messages using a classification code or using *de novo* categories;
- analysing the content of messages using metaphors;
- analysing the patterns of interactions between community members;
- identifying critical incidents and exploring these, for example by narrative analysis of messages or through interviews (virtual, by phone, or face-to-face) with community members.

A common approach to narrative analysis is to identify and analyse the content of messages, transcripts, questionnaires or interviews and the purpose of this is to identify significant themes or issues within the community. There are two distinct approaches to this work, that is the use of a classification code or *de novo* categories. Vic Lally (2002a) provides an example of a classification code where he codes messages into categories based on the type of learning illustrated in the messages as follows:

Type of learning
- Cognitive
- Affective
- Metacognitive
- Miscellaneous

Using this type of coding scheme provides the following summary of learning

Table 11.4 Summary of learning activities as represented in discussion board messages

| Type of learning | Community member learning activities (% number of messages) | | | | | | |
	Jane	Bushra	Chris	John	Sam	Anne	TOTAL
Cognitive	8	12	2	6	15	11	54
Affective	2	4	1	2	8	5	22
Metacognitive	2	3	0	3	4	3	15
Miscellaneous	0	1	3	1	2	2	9
TOTAL	12	20	6	12	29	21	100

activities as represented in the messages posted in the community. This summary indicates different levels of activity as indicated in Table 11.4, for example Bushra, Sam and Anne are clearly actively participating in the learning activities and this is in sharp contrast to Chris whose level of engagement is much lower.

Vic Lally describes some of the challenges of this type of analysis which in addition to being time-consuming and cumbersome, involves a '. . . balance between over-simplification, resulting in the loss of subtlety and insight into complex processes and over-coding where the themes and trends are obscured by too many sub-categories'. Another approach to coding of content is to use *de novo* categories, that is categories that are identified from the messages themselves rather than those based on a theoretical framework. One of the authors (Allan 2004) devised a coding scheme to identify the content of e-learners' messages with respect to time and to plot these over the life of the community. The coding scheme was developed based on the findings from a pilot questionnaire and contained 12 categories (see Table 11.5). This schema was used to analyse an initial 30 messages. However, it did not work as it was over-complex and it was difficult to match the codes with the content of the messages.

So the coding schema was simplified to two codes: reflection and management. In practice this simple scheme worked well and was used on the first eight threads of three groups of e-learners and a total of 1140 messages

Table 11.5 Initial *de novo* coding scheme

	Coded as:	
Style of time management	Planned	Opportunistic
Approach to time	Clock	Natural
Driver	Internal	External
Outcomes	Met	Not met
Main focus	Learning community	Elsewhere
Feelings	Positive	Negative

were analysed. Messages where the content illustrated that the e-learner was exploring their approach to time and time management issues with respect to their online work were coded as 'reflection' and messages that indicated that the e-learner was organizing time, for example arranging online meetings with their colleagues were coded as 'management'. If both types of comment were made in one message then they were coded both 'reflection' and 'management'. The findings were then tabulated and plotted in a graph as shown in Figure 9.1 (page 152). This type of data analysis and presentation can be facilitated with the help of computer-assisted data anlaysis software such as CAQDAS.

Another approach to narrative analysis is to identify and utilize metaphors as a way to 'get under the surface' and understanding the experiences of community members. One of the authors (Allan 2004) used metaphor to explore the learners' subjective experiences with respect to time and this

Table 11.6 Classification of metaphors used by community members

Approach to time	*Illustrative metaphors*
Time as a scarce commodity	'I'm really short of time.'
	'I too am having difficulty finding enough time to do anything other than "read the messages and run", and it is not through any lack of enthusiasm or interest, I'm just too darn busy at the moment. I'm hoping things will get slightly less busy soon.'
Challenges in managing time	'I find the same problems as some of you, in scheduling a regular time slot to do justice to the activity.'
	'It's a problem planning a time when you can access the environment and getting into a routine and sticking to it.'
Conflict between natural study patterns and external factors	'In particular, whilst I like to work at my own pace I'm finding it difficult to schedule time for this – a situation exacerbated because I don't have a PC and web access at home and I guess I've always been a night owl student.'
	'I've always had an issue with course and assignment timetables on formal courses because sometimes it feels like just as your're comfortably and happily immersed in a favourite aspect of a topic and feel comfortable, there is an antagonistic pressure to come out and focus on other topics/modules.'
Lack of control	'The timing hampered us a lot I think – the run up to Christmas is always a mad time and people just don't have the space to suddenly start working on a project like this. Because of other commitments I think the group found it hard to get going on anything constructive – we spent a lot of time just trying to find out if we could all talk together let alone work together.'

involved a painstaking manual search through 1140 messages (from 57 members of three distinct learning communities) and it resulted in the identification of 30 metaphors relating to time. These metaphors were grouped according to their underlying themes as listed in Table 11.6. The use of these metaphors does help to illustrate the community members' experiences of time and it provided a sense of the subjective experience of individual members.

The analysis of narrative using coding schema or metaphors provides insights into the main themes and issues of a community. However, these approaches don't illustrate participation patterns of community members. The analysis of patterns of interactions between community members involves collecting and collating data such as:

- total number of messages written per participant;
- number of people who have read a particular message from a particular person;
- number of messages a person has read from others.

In addition networks can be built up showing the interrelationships of people, for example member A normally responds to messages from members B, C and D but not from member E.

Results of evaluation

The results of the evaluation process may be presented in a number of different ways, for example a report or conference paper, and this will then be disseminated to the appropriate people. The example shown in Box 11.3 is a feedback document summarizing participant feedback and facilitator action taken at the end of the first phase of a virtual learning community. This simple proforma ensured that the loop between participant feedback and facilitator action was completed; this process of ongoing evaluation and action is an integral feature of the quality assurance of learning communities within the organization concerned.

Box 11.3   Virtual learning community: Phase 1 – Evaluation summary

Facilitator and participants – summary and actions

TITLE: Learning community phase one
DATE: 14/3/02

Participant points raised	Facilitator action taken
1. Initial induction event contained a session on WebCT and problems arose in this due to password and other technical difficulties.	1. Suggest that in future programmes a separate introduction to WebCT is organized and led by Information Technology staff.

	More emphasis to be placed on a carefully guided induction process.
2. Initial WebCT site was unclear.	2. This was modified as the community developed.
3. The initial schedule was over-ambitious and needed to be amended.	3. We reduced the number of activities and also provided a longer time for participants to complete these activities. Phase 2 was amended to take into account this feedback.
4. Many participants experienced stress due to time pressures which were in part caused by the over-ambitious schedule and they were also caused by their heavy workloads and lack of time off from normal work duties.	4. See 3 above. Situation needs to be picked up within departments.
5. Absence of mentors during Phase 1 meant that participants lacked additional support and guidance.	5. Mentors have been appointed.
6. Guest speaker – this was a disappointing experience. The guest speaker while conscientious in his contributions to the group failed to motivate and enthuse the participants.	6. Facilitators to provide more detailed guidance to guest speakers and also to draw up a set of guidelines for guest speakers.
7. Some people thought there was too little guidance on reading.	7. Once this issue was identified then learning resources were identified as either essential or supplementary reading.

The findings from the evaluation process may result in a number of different outcomes:

- The virtual learning community is abandoned.
- The virtual learning community is re-designed – new members, facilitators, goals, learning processes.
- The support structures are modified or changed, for example new administrative processes, new learning environment.
- No change.

Researching into virtual learning communities

There is an increasingly large body of research into networked learning communities and many practitioners are actively engaged in this activity as a means of developing their knowledge about networked learning communities. The existence of messages posted by community members and also transcripts of chat room sessions means that it is relatively easy to access information about community members and their activities. There is an important ethical dimension in carrying out this type of research and it is important for the researcher to consider ethical issues and obtain consent from community members and their sponsors. Box 11.4 contains an example research consent form. Methods used to protect participants include the importance of maintaining member anonymity and confidentiality. In this book individual names and, in some instances, organizational allegiance have been changed to protect individuals. In addition some details have been changed to ensure that the notion of confidentiality is upheld.

Box 11.4   Example research consent form

Title:
Principal investigator:
Co-investigator:
Description of research participants:

Purpose

Overall aim

Evaluation objectives
We would like permission to use questionnaires, individual and focus group interviews and online discussion materials (discussion messages, conference transcripts, e-mails) in this ongoing research project.

Procedures

The research methodology includes:

- Analysis of participation data
- Use of case studies
- Analysis of content of postings, transcripts or e-mails
- Individual interviews lasting no longer than 30 minutes and at a mutually negotiated venue or by telephone focus group interviews lasting no longer than 1 hour and 30 minutes and at a mutually negotiated venue

---

Any data that we use will be:

- Summarized to demonstrate overall patterns of participation
- Anonymous and confidential, i.e. any distinguishing names, details or other identifying information will be deleted from any examples or case studies

Permission

- Individual permission will be sought to use direct quotes or examples

Confidentiality

The results of this study may be: used to inform a final report, published in a book or journal or used for teaching purposes. However, your name or other identifiers will not be used in any publication or teaching materials without your specific permission.

Request for more information

You may ask more questions about the study at any time. The investigator(s) will provide their telephone number(s) so that they are available to answer your questions or concerns about the study. You will be informed of any significant new findings discovered during the course of this study that might influence your continued participation. A copy of this consent form will be given to you to keep.

Refusal or withdrawal of participation

Participation in this study is voluntary. You do not have to participate in this study. Your present or future benefits if entitled will not be affected should you choose not to participate. If you decide to participate, you can change your mind and drop out of the study at any time without affecting your present or future affiliation at the university and any benefits if entitled.

Consent statement

I give permission for my contributions to the online activities as part of the ************ to be used in this research project. I understand that I can withdraw this permission at any time leading up to the publication of the research project findings.

Printed name   Signature

E-mail   Date

Summary

Evaluation is an essential element of facilitating virtual learning communities. Standard evaluation tools such as questionnaires, interviews and focus groups may be used as part of the evaluation process. In addition, the virtual communication arena provides a rich source of data and will provide detailed statistics on participation levels. The content of discussion group messages and conference transcripts may be analysed using a variety of techniques including coding and metaphor analysis. The evaluation process enables members, facilitators, managers and other stakeholders to learn from the experiences of the virtual learning community and improve their practice.

References

Allan, B. (2002) *E-learning and Teaching in Library and Information Services*. London: Facet Publishing.

Allan, B. (2004) E-learners experiences of time, in: S. Banks, *et al.* (eds) (2004) *Networked Learning 2004*, 5–7 April, University of Lancaster, Lancaster, pp. 341–47.

Allan, B., Barker, M., Fairburn, K., Freeman, M. and Sutherland, P. (2002) High level student autonomy in a virtual learning environment, *Networked Learning 2002: A research-based conference on e-learning in higher education and lifelong learning*. University of Sheffield, Sheffield, UK, 26–28 March.

Belbin, M. (1993) *Team Roles at Work*. Oxford: Butterworth-Heinemann.

Brophy, P. (2002) The evaluation of public library online services: measuring impact, *The People's Network Workshop Series Issue Papers* No. 1. Available at: www.peoplesnetwork.gov.uk (accessed on 23/07/03).

Collins, A., Brown, J.S. and Newman, S. (1989) Cognitive apprenticeship, in L.B. Resnick, (ed.), *Knowing, Learning and Instruction: Essays in Honour of Richard Glasser*. Hillsdale, NJ: Lawrence Erlbaum Associates, Inc., pp. 453–94.

Cooper, T. and Smith, B. (2000) Reflecting and learning from experience of online tuition: implications for staff development and quality assurance processes to support learner learning in this medium. Open University Millennium Conference proceedings.

Corrall, S. (1999) Knowledge management: Are we in the knowledge management business? *Ariadne*, 18. Available at: http://www.ariadne.ac.uk/issue18/knowledge-mgt/ (accessed on 24/05/04).

Cox, S. *et al.* (2000) How to herd cats in Piccadilly, *Times Higher Education Supplement*, 14 April, pp. 36–7.

Dakers, H. (2003) The BL reaches out, *Library and Information Update*, 2(10): 46–7.

Darrouzet, C. and Lynn, C. (1999) *Creating a New Architecture for Learning*. Summary of the outcomes of the Asian Bank Capability Building Workshop, 9–18 August, Tokyo, Japan, pp. 674–81. Available at: http://www2.nesu.edu/unity/lockers/users/f/felder/public/ILSpage.html (accessed on 26/06/02).

Daugaard, V. (2003) The co-operation across cultures in public and scientific libraries: The co-operation in Net Librarian, *World Library and Information Congress: 69th IFLA General Conference and Council*, 1–9 August, Berlin. Available at http://www.ifla.org (accessed on 25/09/03).

Dillenbourg, P. (1999) What do you mean by collaborative learning? in P. Dillenbourg (ed.), *Collaborative-learning: Cognitive and Computational Approaches*, pp. 1–16. London: Elsevier.

Garratt, T. (1997) *The Effective Delivery of Training using NLP*. London: Kogan Page.

Goodyear, P. (2000) Effective networked learning in higher education: notes and guidelines, Networked learning in Higher Education (JISC/CALT). Available from: http://csalt.lancs.ac.uk/jisc (accessed on 23/02/03).

Harris, C. (2002) Experience of running collaborative projects: Report to the Research Support Libraries Programme. Available on: http://www.rslp.ac.uk (accessed on 23/02/04).

Headlam-Wells, J. *et al.* (2004) *E-mentoring for Women's Careers and Management Development*. Hull: University of Hull Business School.

Hislop, G. (2000) Working professionals as part-time on-line learners, *JALN* 4(2). Available at: http://www.aln.org/publications/jaln/v4n2/v4n2_hislop.asp (accessed on 12/04/02).

INSPIRAL (2001) *Definitions*. Available at: http://Inspiral.cdlr.strath.ac.uk/about/vlemle.html (accessed on 23/05/04).

Jensen, E. (1996) *Brain-Based Learning and Teaching*. Del Mar, CA: Turning Point Publishing.

Jonassen, D.H. (1995) Learning strategies: A new educational technology, *Programmed Learning and Educational Technology*, 22(1): 26–34.

Jones, S. *et al.* (2000) Establishing on-line communities for school leaders. An interim report. Available at: http://www.ultralab.net/papers/bera2001/th/bera2001th.pdf (accessed 23/05/04).

Kearsley, G. and Shneiderman, B. (1998) Engagement theory: a framework for technology-based teaching and learning, *Educational Technology*, September/October: 20–37.

Lally, V. (2002a) Deciphering individual learning processes in virtual professional development, *Networked Learning 2002: A research-based conference on e-learning in higher education and lifelong learning*. University of Sheffield, Sheffield, UK. 26–28 March. Available on: http://www.shef.ac.uk/nlc2002/ (accessed on 07/01/04).

Lally, V. (2002b) Squaring the circle: triangulating content and social network analysis with critical event recall. *Networked Learning 2002: A research-based conference on e-learning in higher education and lifelong learning*. University of Sheffield, Sheffield, UK. 26–28 March. Available on: http://www.shef.ac.uk/nlc2002/ (accessed on 07/01/04).

Lave, J. and Wenger, E. (1991) *Situated Learning. Legitimate Peripheral Participation*, Cambridge: Cambridge University Press.

Littlejohn, A. and Higginson, C. (2003) A Guide for Teachers. LTSN Generic Centre – E-learning Series. Learning and Teaching Support Network. Available at www.ltsn.ac.uk

Malhotra, Y. (2004) Why knowledge management systems fail? Enablers and constraints of knowledge management in human enterprises, in Michael E.D. Koenig and T. Kanti Srikantaiah (eds), *Knowledge Management Lessons Learned: What Works and What Doesn't*, Information Today Inc. (American Society for Information Science and Technology Monograph Series): 87–112.

McCabe, M.F. (1998) Lessons from the field: computer conferencing in higher education, *Journal of Information Technology for Teacher Education*, 7(1): 71–88.

McConnell, D. (2000) *Implementing Computer Supported Cooperative Learning*. London: Kogan Page.

McDermott, R. (2000) Community development as a natural step, *Knowledge Management Review*, 3(5): 6–19.

Nickols, F. (2000) *Communities of Practice Overview*. Available at: home.att.net/~nickols/articles.htm (accessed on 15/01/03).

Nonaka, I. (1991) The knowledge creating company, *Harvard Business Review*, 69(6): 96–104.

Panitz, T. (1999) A definition of collaborative vs cooperative learning. http://www.lgu.ac.uk/deliberations/collab.learning/panitz2.html (accessed on 03/10/03).

Rochelle, J. and Teasley, S.D. (1995) The construction of shared knowledge in collaborative problem solving, in C. O'Mailley (ed.), *Computer Supported Collaborative Learning*, pp. 69–97. Berlin: Springer.

Salmon, G. (2002) *E-moderating*. London: Kogan Page.

Sullivan, H. and Skelcher, C. (2002) *Working Across Boundaries*. Basingstoke: Palgrave, Macmillan.

Van Ryneveld, L. (no date) What is Constructivism? Available at: http://hagar.up.ac.za/catts/learner/lindavr/lindapg1 htm (accessed on 19/03/01).

Vygotsky, L.S. (1978) *Mind in Society: The Development of Higher Psychological Processes*. Cambridge, MA: Harvard University Press.

Wang, F-K. and Bonk, C.J. (2001) A design framework for electronic cognitive apprenticeship, *JALN*, 5(2). Available from: http://www.aln.org/publications/jaln/v5n2/pdf/ (accessed on 27/01/03).

Ward, S. (1999) Information professionals for the next millennium, *Journal of Information Science*, 25(4): 239–47.

Wenger, E. (1998) *Communities of Practice: Learning, Meaning and Identity*. Cambridge: Cambridge University Press.

Wenger, E., McDermott, R. and Snyder, W. (2002) *Cultivating Communities of Practice*. Boston: Harvard Businesss School Press.

Wilson, B. and Ryder, M. (1996) *Dynamic Learning Communities: An Alternative to Designed Instructional System*. Available at: http://carbon.cudenver.edu/~mryder/dlc.html (accessed 12/03/03).

Index

The Society for Research into Higher Education

The Society for Research into Higher Education (SRHE), an international body, exists to stimulate and coordinate research into all aspects of higher education. It aims to improve the quality of higher education through the encouragement of debate and publication on issues of policy, on the organization and management of higher education institutions, and on the curriculum, teaching and learning methods.

The Society is entirely independent and receives no subsidies, although individual events often receive sponsorship from business or industry. The Society is financed through corporate and individual subscriptions and has members from many parts of the world. It is an NGO of UNESCO.

Under the imprint *SRHE & Open University Press*, the Society is a specialist publisher of research, having over 80 titles in print. In addition to *SRHE News*, the Society's newsletter, the Society publishes three journals: *Studies in Higher Education* (three issues a year), *Higher Education Quarterly* and *Research into Higher Education Abstracts* (three issues a year).

The Society runs frequent conferences, consultations, seminars and other events. The annual conference in December is organized at and with a higher education institution. There are a growing number of networks which focus on particular areas of interest, including:

Access	FE/HE
Assessment	Graduate Employment
Consultants	New Technology for Learning
Curriculum Development	Postgraduate Issues
Eastern European	Quantitative Studies
Educational Development Research	Student Development

Benefits to members

Individual

- The opportunity to participate in the Society's networks
- Reduced rates for the annual conferences
- Free copies of *Research into Higher Education Abstracts*
- Reduced rates for *Studies in Higher Education*

- Reduced rates for *Higher Education Quarterly*
- Free online access to *Register of Members' Research Interests* – includes valuable reference material on research being pursued by the Society's members
- Free copy of occasional in-house publications, e.g. *The Thirtieth Anniversary Seminars Presented by the Vice-Presidents*
- Free copies of *SRHE News* and *International News* which inform members of the Society's activities and provides a calendar of events, with additional material provided in regular mailings
- A 35 per cent discount on all SRHE/Open University Press books
- The opportunity for you to apply for the annual research grants
- Inclusion of your research in the *Register of Members' Research Interests*

Corporate

- Reduced rates for the annual conference
- The opportunity for members of the Institution to attend SRHE's network events at reduced rates
- Free copies of *Research into Higher Education Abstracts*
- Free copies of *Studies in Higher Education*
- Free online access to *Register of Members' Research Interests* – includes valuable reference material on research being pursued by the Society's members
- Free copy of occasional in-house publications
- Free copies of *SRHE News* and *International News*
- A 35 per cent discount on all SRHE/Open University Press books
- The opportunity for members of the Institution to submit applications for the Society's research grants
- The opportunity to work with the Society and co-host conferences
- The opportunity to include in the *Register of Members' Research Interests* your Institution's research into aspects of higher education

Membership details: SRHE, 76 Portland Place, London W1B 1NT, UK Tel: 020 7637 2766. Fax: 020 7637 2781. email: srheoffice@srhe.ac.uk
world wide web: http://www.srhe.ac.uk./srhe/
Catalogue: SRHE & Open University Press, McGraw-Hill Education, McGraw-Hill House, Shoppenhangers Road, Maidenhead, Berkshire SL6 2QL. Tel: 01628 502500. Fax: 01628 770224. email: enquiries@openup.co.uk –
web: www.openup.co.uk

Related books from Open University Press
Purchase from www.openup.co.uk or order through your local bookseller

FOUNDATIONS OF PROBLEM-BASED LEARNING

Maggi Savin-Baden and Claire Howell Major

Despite the growth in the use of problem-based learning since it was first popularized by Barrows and Tamblyn (1980) in the first book on the subject, no text has examined the foundations of the approach nor offered straightforward guidance to those wishing to explore, understand, and implement it. This book describes the theoretical foundations of problem-based learning and is a practical source for staff wanting to implement it.

The book is designed as a text that not only explores the foundations of problem-based learning and but also answers many of the often-asked questions about its use. It has also been designed to develops the reader's understanding beyond implementation, including issues such as academic development, cultural, diversity, assessment, evaluation and curricular models of problem-based learning.

Contents
*Acknowledgements – Prologue – **Part 1: Conceptual frames** – Delineating core concepts of problem-based learning – A brief history of problem-based learning – Problem-based learning and theories of learning – Curricula models – Cultural contexts of academe – **Part 2: Recurring themes** – What is a problem? – Learning teams – The role of students – The role of tutor – Staff support and development – Assessing problem-based learning – **Part 3: Broadening horizons** – Embracing culture and diversity – Programme evaluation – Sustaining problem-based learning curricula – Epilogue: Future imperative? – Glossary – Bibliography – Index.*

224pp   0 335 21531 9 (Paperback)   0 335 21532 7 (Hardback)

PUTTING THE UNIVERSITY ONLINE
INFORMATION, TECHNOLOGY, AND ORGANIZATIONAL CHANGE

James Cornford and Neil Pollock

- What kind of university is emerging from the widespread adoption of new information and communication technologies in teaching, research and administration?
- What is the nature and scale of the work required to put the university online?
- What are the consequences – for academics, students, managers and others – of putting the university online?

New information and communication technologies (ICTs), and above all the internet, hold out many promises for higher education institutions in terms of flexibility, efficiency, quality and access. The vision is that of a virtual institution. *Putting the University Online* seeks to uncover what the pursuit of that vision means for an institution, its staff, students and other stakeholders, and consequences, intended and unintended, for the role and identity of the university.

This is the first book length study, based on detailed fine-grained analysis of what 'putting the university online' actually means for those involved and the wider institutions. James Cornford and Neil Pollock draw both on theories from the sociology of technology and on a large and diverse body of empirical research in order to explore how universities are attempting to build and use new ICTs to sit alongside, complement and, in some cases, replace established means of delivering, organizing and managing higher education. Their book will help sensitize policy makers, academics, university managers, and students to the limits to, and implications of, the pursuit of a virtual future for higher education.

Contents
The role of technology within universities – The 'work' of building the virtual university – The university campus as a 'resourceful constraint' – The virtual university is the university made concrete – The informational view of universities – Enterprise-wide systems and the university as an 'unique' organization – Campus management and the 'self-service' student – Conclusions – References – Index.

144pp   0 335 21005 8 (Paperback)   0 335 21006 6 (Hardback)